Out of

INDIA

Out of

INDIA

A true story about
the New Age movement

Caryl Matrisciana

Revised and adapted from the best-selling
book and film *Gods of the New Age*

Lighthouse Trails Publishing
Eureka, Montana

Out of India

© **2008 Caryl Matrisciana**
First Edition, 3rd Printing, 2014
Published by:
Lighthouse Trails Publishing
Eureka, Montana
(see back of book for publisher and author contact information)

For photo and illustration credits, please see page 231.
For song and lyric credits, please see page 233.

Library of Congress Cataloging-in-Publication Data

Matrisciana, Caryl, 1947-
  Out of India : a true story about the New Age movement / Caryl Matrisciana. -- 1st ed.
  ISBN: 978-0-9791315-3-0 (softbound : alk. paper)
  1. Cults. 2. Matrisciana, Caryl, 1947- 3. New Age movement. I. Title.
  BP603.M297 2008
  261.2'4--dc22

                                        2008012805

Out of India is a revised and expanded edition of *Gods of the New Age* (Harvest House, 1985).

Note: Lighthouse Trails Publishing books are available at special quantity discounts. Contact information for publisher in back of book.

Printed in the United States of America

Dedication

To the loving memories of my Dad and Mum who afforded me the upbringing I deeply cherish. And, to the Lord Jesus Christ Who rescued me from spiritual deception into His eternal life and light.

Contents

PART TWO: A NEW AGE/NEW SPIRITUALITY
East Comes West—1970s - 21st Century

PART ONE

FROM DARKNESS INTO LIGHT
1950s –1960s

When I was twenty years old, my family returned from India, where I was born and lived for most of my life, to England, our homeland. It was during the turbulent sixties, and I was about to be introduced to a movement that didn't even have a name yet. How could I have possibly known then that the strange and mystical religion I had been surrounded by in India would someday be at the heart of a spirituality that would influence millions around the world?

One

Bus Ride to the Future

I will never forget that hot, muggy day in London in the summer of 1966 when I was twenty years old. How *could* I forget? After all, it was the day that changed my life forever.

Perhaps if I had been out in the English countryside or beside the sea, that hot, stifling day would have been bearable—but in the city it was miserable. Oh, to be in a garden with its soothing assortment of colorful flowers, my feet dangling in a cool spring!

Reality was all too blatant. The British capital was steeped and simmering in its own crowded bustle, intense noise, and pandemonium of traffic. By day's end I could hardly bear the sound and sweat of it all as I was jostled along in an overcrowded, red, double-decker bus through rush-hour traffic.

Still, in spite of all the unpleasantness, a breathless anticipation filled my soul. That surging excitement was my only motivation to struggle across blistering-hot London. I knew I was on my way to a marvelous experience.

Eventually the bus rounded Piccadilly Circus and honked

impatiently at the myriads of pedestrians overflowing onto the streets. The sidewalk vendors and little shops were teeming with hundreds of tourists. T-shirts hanging on shop canopies sported the slogan "swinging London," along with coffee mugs, postcards, and dozens of other souvenir items.

A New Spiritual Gospel

The phrase "swinging London" had recently been splashed across the world's newsstands by *Time* magazine[1] and had captured an atmosphere that really did permeate the London air. I basked proudly in the energy that surrounded me, enchanted with the good fortune to live and work in this pulsating metropolis.

The bus changed gears noisily and puffed out dirty diesel fumes. We moved slowly down Shaftesbury Avenue, the heart of theater land, in Soho. My pulse pounded harder. The next stop was my destination.

I pushed my way through the crowded bus and jumped off with a spurt of enthusiasm. Renewed vigor had me effortlessly nudging my way through throngs of theater goers who crowded

A double-decker London bus

the sidewalks. At last I arrived! I stood still for what seemed to be an endless moment, absorbing the glowing neon advertisements that assured me I was at the right place. The theater marquee carried but one word. The name of the show was *Hair*.[2]

Soon I was to experience the musical blockbuster that the whole world was singing about. The people milling around me were quite different in appearance from those on the bus. Denim jeans, casual Indian cotton shirts, and hippie informality identified almost everyone. Hairstyles ranged from long to longer to longest. I grinned to myself, realizing I too looked like the *in* generation. At the same time, it was a relief to know that my parents couldn't see me now. How they would argue that I was not conforming to the "required London theater dress."

I had waited months for tonight. Tickets for *Hair* were nearly impossible to buy. I clutched mine protectively, waiting to squeeze through the door. Scanning the crowd, I searched for the friends I was to meet.

The air buzzed as people hummed various songs from the score that was about to begin. Never before had I gone into a show already so familiar with its lyrics and tunes. For months the airwaves had carried those melodies around the world.

Still, I could not have imagined the impact the show itself was to have on my life and thinking. I would not have guessed how religiously I would follow this new spiritual "gospel." I was about to be "converted" by the message of *Hair*, along with thousands of other people of my generation.

We shuffled inside and located our seats. The theater darkened. The rustle of programs stilled. Chills and goose bumps spread through the audience as the orchestra began to play. There was heavy, loud rock music as magnificent, full voices swelled in harmony. There were colors, lights, and sounds. Everything mingled together to draw me willingly, passionately, into the phenomenon. Never before had I known such intense involvement in a theatrical production.

With exciting extravagance, the show animated and popularized outrageously impudent and risqué ideas. Tricky little songs whipped us into attitudes of rebellion and promiscuity. We cheered and applauded the demise of family, society, government, and country. We decried the past and its values. We sang about the hopeless state of our planet; we coughed and choked for the pollution and wept over the sadness of war.

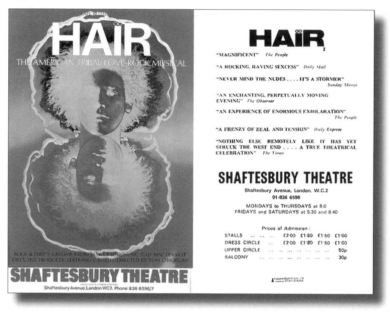

Handbill for the London *Hair* production at Shaftesbury Theatre

Every person in the audience was transformed into a mystical searcher through the song lyrics. Everyone contemplated the plaintive question asked in, "Where Do I Go?" That particular song had us following everything, nothing, and even *myself*. It had us asking the eternal question posed in the lyrics, "And will I ever discover why I live and die?"[3]

Like many other people my age, I had never considered that topic before, but I was to do so a thousand times in the days and months to come. That evening's performance was to lead me, and countless others, on a spiritual quest.

Having disparaged the past and present and looking grimly into the emptiness of no solution, *Hair* suddenly gave a glimmer of hope. We whooped ecstatically through the marvelous escape presented in "Hashish." This gleeful song promoted the *wow* experience one could achieve through no less than twenty-five different highs.

In the years to come, I would get hooked on one particular high and try several others. I would understand all too well the appeal of replacing realism with psychedelia.

A New Way of Thinking

L ittle did I comprehend at the time that through this musical I was being subtly introduced to a new religious system. One song ridiculed the faith of my youth. It encouraged us not to believe in God per se, but instead, to see that we ourselves were like gods. Joyfully we sang the immortal words of the great poet William Shakespeare, taken from his play *Hamlet*:

> What a piece of work man is!
> How noble in reason, how infinite in faculty.
> In form and moving, how express and admirable, In action how like an angel,
> In apprehension how like a god.[4]

My perception of the world was about to change. From here on I was being introduced to a new alternative to my old way of life—one that in the future was to jealously lead me into an uncompromising spiritual dimension.

"Let the sunshine in," the cast vocalized.[5]

"Let the sunshine in!" we responded at the tops of our voices. *Oh yes, oh yes! Let the sunshine in!* My heart ached with hope. How I longed to experience this new "opening" and its promised sensation. In any case, it would have been hopeless to struggle against the overpowering emotional, mental, and sensual seduction taking place.

We were enticed to taste the fruits of another consciousness through drugs. In exciting harmony we were invited to *lock the doors* of our minds and *pull down the blinds*... "total self-awareness the intention."[6]

Those lyrics sent us traveling into our bodies and into inner worlds. We were led through guided imagery, visualization, rhythmic music, and enthusiastic energy—to merge with the universe. Through powerful suggestion, colors meshed and individuals joined together in one cosmic force—a force I eventually learned to call "God."

Our souls could be released from our bodies through astral projection and joined to this "God." Coming into his presence, we touched him! "Oh, my God," I hummed with the cast, "your skin is soft, I love your face." I wept quietly in ecstasy. In my euphoric state, my mind was lulled and led by the musical through many scenes and ideas. And those that made the deepest impression on me were the ones that led through the paths of India. It wasn't so much that I could relate to the spiritual alternatives that were proclaimed in song; it was that the land of India was in my heart. I had lived there for much of the past nineteen years. I had been born there and considered it my real home.

Ironically, at this point my familiarity with India began to trouble me a bit. I was mildly disturbed as *Hair* took a new turn. The stage filled with the musical sounds of my youth—sitar twangs and skin drum beats. Vibrant music accompanied worshipers of Krishna (one of the millions of India's gods) onto the stage. Clashing cymbals, hypnotic rhythm, and melodic chants encouraged us to repeat "Hare Krishna, Hare Krishna!" I felt reluctant. Nervously I looked around, but most of the audience joined in. They seemed unaware that they were praying. They didn't realize they were invoking and praising an Indian deity.

Krishna disciples were not entirely new to any of us. They had been a high-profile curiosity on Oxford Street, London's shopping center, for months as they moved with vigor among the shop goers and tourists. I see now that the saffron-clad devotees so glamorously portrayed on stage gave the group a respectability that changed its future mission in the West. This would eventually bring thousands of converts into its ranks.

Even in Bengal, where I had spent most of my growing years, this sect (which was established there in the fifteenth century A.D.) did not display the sort of fanatic trancelike madness that we witnessed on Oxford Street or on the stage of *Hair*. I wondered why Westerners were so enthralled with a religious activity that didn't incite much enthusiasm even among its own people in India?

The show moved along captivatingly. In the same way that the Hare Krishna sect was glorified, suddenly so was Yoga. *Yoga!* Alarm bells rang in my mind. The Yoga I had seen in India was intense, arduous, and serious—a discipline taught by avowed spiritual masters who prepared their disciples for death. So why did *Hair*'s hero in the song "Donna" go to India to see the *Yoga light?* Why was it associated with drugs and reincarnation and presented as such a sweet, new spiritual experience?

I was more than a little confused now. In India, I had understood reincarnation as a terrible prison with no escape. Now I heard this young man sing that he was reincarnated and so were we all!

Here he was, recalling all his mystical experiences in India—Yoga, reincarnation, and drugs—and telling us this would help us "evolve," to develop, to unfold and open.

I wanted desperately to belong to this energy—even if it meant giving up the old and embracing the new (although I didn't really understand it), even if it meant turning to concepts I thought were strange and weird and perhaps even wrong. The result would be worth it!

Besides, I told myself, *maybe the concepts aren't wrong; maybe they are just different. Maybe my protected upbringing in boarding school and my sheltered life in India were too narrow.* I wondered why I had somehow missed seeing all these important mystical aspects of India. Why could I only remember the tragedy, the poverty, the disease, the cruelty, and the apathy? Surely all these people here tonight couldn't be wrong. I wrestled with my heart and soul to uncritically accept all I was hearing, seeing, and feeling. I longed to capture this excitement for myself.

The performers were charged with enthusiasm. They jumped off the stage and mingled with the audience—for me, a theatrical first. It was overwhelming to have them touch us, singing and dancing around us. Now they encouraged us to join in the anthem "Aquarius."

That familiar song brought me back to the performance with a jolt—

> When the moon is in the Seventh House,
> And Jupiter aligns with Mars
> Then peace will guide the planets,
> And love will steer the stars.
> This is the dawning of the Age of Aquarius! . . .
>
> Harmony and understanding,
> Sympathy and trust abounding
> No more falsehoods or derisions
> Golden living dreams of visions,
> Mystic crystal revelation,
> And the mind's true liberation
> Aquarius! Aquarius[7]

The show was over. Soon the theater stage was dark. But my spiritual journey in search of light was just beginning.

For some time to come, the strains of "Aquarius" grew louder and more distinct among young people throughout Western culture. That song summed up the newly-born hopes of a generation: its lyrics clearly stated the hope and vision of the New Age.

Today, like never before, our planet is filled with desperate people, facing the problem of an ever-deteriorating world. On one hand, man is disillusioned with himself, but on the other, he is ever searching for answers in technology and other expressions of *human potential*. He dreams that a more fully evolved, enlightened human specimen will establish a utopian world, one with a perfect political and social system, without disease, poverty, or suffering.

Years ago, *Hair* prophesied that this Utopia would come through occult, mystical realms. Our direction would come

Hair cast photo singing "I Got Life" on Broadway—1970

through dreams and visions, through mystic revelation, and through the stars (astrology).

A far more developed belief system, a far more aggressive group of leaders, and a far more determined mass of followers has become what is known as the New Age movement. *Hair's* visionaries couldn't have hoped for more.

Now I look back and realize the devastating impact that *Hair's* message had on my thinking, religious outlook, attitudes, and morality. *Hair* not only led me, and millions like me worldwide, into a new mode of rationalizing, it conditioned and honed us for things to come. *Hair* represented the foundational ideas that prepared us and our world for the principles that underlie today's most influential mindset—New Age thinking.

The Age of Aquarius and a Promise of Peace

Millions of people who are being influenced by the New Age do not realize they are being conditioned by a powerful religious and political structure: globalism is the goal, and peace is the promise.

I remember endless conversations with peers in the '60s who

were predominantly focused on hopeless gloom. With unrelenting paranoia, we discussed the inadequacies of society. "Everything," we agreed, "is corrupt." This included medicine, food, environment, politics, and education.

A cultivated atmosphere of fear and doom forced us to escape into our own man-made solutions, since answers could only come from us, the awareness brigade, and our enlightened alternatives. Like millions of others, we concluded that a new world order was our only salvation. Our spiritual resources, if encouraged and tapped correctly, could bring goodness, harmony and peace to the world.

The results of nearly fifty years of New Age infiltration into the Western world are staggering. In 1980, Marilyn Ferguson, a major New Age prophetess, wrote a veritable manifesto of New Age philosophy titled *The Aquarian Conspiracy*. Explaining the choice of title for her best seller, she says this:

> Conspire, in its literal sense, means "to breathe together." It is an intimate joining. To make clear the benevolent nature of this joining, I chose the word Aquarian . . . after a dark, violent age, the Piscean, we are entering a millennium of love and light—in the words of the popular song, "The Age of Aquarius," the time of "the mind's true liberation."[8]

Although countless arguments will continue to debate the insinuation of New Age thinking into our culture, the consensus is that a widespread shift in consciousness is taking place. And this is displaying itself in our everyday lives, right under our noses!

New Age proponent David Spangler describes this hope of a New Age world:

> The earth [is] entering a new cycle of evolution, which [will be] marked by the appearance of a new consciousness within humanity that would give birth to a new civilization . . . They would then enter a new

age of abundance and spiritual enlightenment—the Age of Aquarius.[9]

This "spiritual enlightenment" can be capsulated in these characteristic points of the New Age:

1. God is seen more as a flowing energy or creative force that exists in all things rather than as a personal God who is distinct from man and creation.
2. Man is seen as divine, essentially a part of God.
3. *Salvation for the soul* is something attained when one becomes an awakened soul by understanding one's divinity and oneness with all. This *awakening* comes about through the use of various rituals and mystical practices that help remove one's attachment to the world.
4. The gap between good and evil is eradicated. In other words, there is no evil—all is divine.

The New Age offers new ideas of peace, love, integrity, and community—all that a needy world is hungry for. It attempts to reform religious ideals based on Judeo-Christian principles with an improved formula of application. It seeks to replace age-old sentiments of patriotism and traditional moral standards with a new philosophy. All of the old-fashioned ideals are dismissed as mundane and archaic.

It also casts the more serious charge that the "old ways" only serve to impede the progress of a society bent on an upward evolution to a higher consciousness—the new power.

The conditioning of a potential New Age disciple may start subconsciously at an early age. Perhaps he is trying to find answers and purposes for his life. A difficult family environment may urge him on. Disillusionments and disappointments may create needs. Dissatisfaction with religious hypocrisy may cause him to explore other philosophies. In my case, all of these contributed to my sense of powerlessness and resultant quest.

I became deeply committed to the New Age agenda, although I

must admit I did not understand the spiritual implications. I merely longed for self-improvement and hungered after some kind of peace and love. In more troubled moments, I sensed a strange recognition of New Age teachings and sometimes felt a disturbing tension to realize that some wonderful new idea of mine had originally been written thousands of years before—in Hindu teachings.

My life experiences had taught me more about India and its religious ramifications than any of my enlightened friends would have dared guess. And in my recollection, nothing to be found along the streets of Calcutta, Bombay, or Madras promised a better life to anyone.

So, in accepting New Age teachings in the 1960s, had I somehow accepted the very religion that had frightened me so much as a child? If so, had I somehow misunderstood the sights and sounds and smells of my childhood?

What were those years in India really like?

Two

India—Through a Child's Eyes

Born in Calcutta, India, March 15, 1947—the last British baby born in British Calcutta before India's Independence.

So begins my baby book. A quick thumb-through discloses photographs of a bright-eyed blond infant seated on various adult laps. Captions read "Caryl, two months old, in Darjeeling" and "Caryl, five months old, in Tollygunge."

Fine clothing and elegant surroundings reveal this is no missionary family's memoirs. So what was a "proper" English child doing in a place like India? The answer is really a lesson in recent Indian history.

British rule was established in India in the 1700s. In the 19th century my great-great-grandmother made the long and tiring journey from England to India with her entire family. This voyage was the result of her father's involvement with the British Diplomatic Service, which became an enormous and integral part of British Imperialism during its 300-year rule in India.

In India, great-great grandmother met and married a fellow Englishman who was eventually to become the Governor-General of Bombay (now called Mumbai). Together they raised their family in the adopted country they had learned to love.

On the other side of my father's family tree, my great-grandfather's clan members in London were the proud caretakers of the River Thames' waterways. Their duties involved overseeing the Royal Barges and, believe it or not, the Royal Swans! In his middle years, my great-grandfather traveled to India on a government commission. He was one of the early pioneers who helped set up India's river-shipping system. These waterways provided for the transportation of exports and eventually became an integral part of that massive trading industry, the famous East India Company.

The next generation, my grandfather's, was actively involved in many of the engineering projects that still stand in India today. Road, rail, and bridge building escalated. By then Britain had succeeded in establishing a strong political unity within India, a land torn apart for centuries by tribal and religious warfare. British armies were drafted to protect the new boarders from feuding

Caryl and her "Mum"

maharajas and their kingdoms. During Grandfather's lifetime, communications suddenly linked that enormous, disjointed country into something resembling a whole. The British colony prospered despite many bureaucratic difficulties.

My great-uncles related countless tales of warfare, murder, and political intrigue. Their reminiscences of the "great ole days in Inja" had me spellbound for hours.

I learned how Christian missionaries brought education to India's illiterate millions, and medicine and health care to a desperately diseased nation.

My relatives told me of the influence Britain's Christian-based tradition was having on some of India's more barbaric cultural customs. Though reforms were slow, customs such as the practice of suttee (wife-burning); bonded slavery; forced child-labor; kidnapping of young boys for cultic use by homosexuals, transvestites, and eunuchs; and human blood sacrifices for religious reasons were at least thwarted.

During World War II, my father journeyed from India to England to enlist in the British Army. While living with his cousins, he met a girl named Bamby who was a friend of the family. Their casual friendship led to regular correspondence through the war years while my father was fighting in Europe and the Middle East. Romance led to marriage in 1946. After a brief honeymoon in Ireland, my father was called back to India by the military.

Although India had been given her independence in August of 1947, the British Army and other aid organizations remained. These were meant to assist India onto her young, independent feet. It was into these circumstances that my mother, by now very pregnant with me, made the laborious sea journey from England's Southampton Docks to my father's home in India.

She traveled against the advice of her doctor and worried family members. They were concerned not only because of her condition but also because she had never before lived in a foreign country, let alone disease-ridden India.

Nevertheless, weeks later, Mother arrived in Calcutta safely, although somewhat dazed by the experience. There she was reunited with my father. There I was born. And there she and I began our encounter with the mysterious East.

A Train Ride in India

My clearest early memories date back to when I was three or four years old. My mind treasures a collection of vividly colored portraits—impressions of distant people and faraway places that never dim with time.

I remember my first adventurous train journey to visit friends in Darjeeling. Nestled in northern India, east of Nepal, this charming hillside resort is world-famous for its aromatic tea and cool, clean mountain air. My mother and I were traveling among many colonial wives and their young families. They took this journey annually to escape the hot summers of the city. Dad, dripping with perspiration, accompanied us to the train. He stood on the crowded railway platform and sadly waved goodbye. We soon left behind the suffocating heat of the city. I remember pressing my face against the cool train window, my eyes eagerly absorbing the stunning countryside, thinking what an exciting adventure it was going to be.

The big train from Calcutta couldn't wend its way up into the mountains, so we had to change trains to climb the final 2000 meters of the trip.

We boarded the rickety "toy" mountain train and chugged our way through dense tropical forests, climbing higher and higher. We passed rich, green tea gardens and terraced rice fields. This area is known as the Land of the White Orchid, and we traveled past myriads of the exotic blooms. Our

mini-train looped through pine-scented groves, past ferns and flower-covered slopes.

After catching glimpses of mist-wrapped snowy peaks, we reached the highest railroad station in the world, Ghoom. Then, making our way down the other side of the mountain, we arrived in beautiful Darjeeling, known by British Colonials as Queen of the Eastern Himalayas. We stopped at the antique Victorian train station and disembarked. Soon we were bustling through the colorful marketplace, rubbing shoulders with the Nepalese, Tibetan, and Bhutanese hill folk who thronged the bazaars.

Met by our friends, we drove past elegant hotels and villas. At last we came to our journey's end—their mountain resort home.

I felt tinier than ever, gazing at the grandeur and beauty of the towering, snow-capped mountains that surround Darjeeling. Many mornings, from famous Tiger Hill, we would witness the unforgettable sight of sunrise over the Himalayan peaks and would watch the dawning shadows turn to a pink glow and slowly light up the snowy summits. Mauve hues would become orange. Suddenly, as the sun pierced the horizon, everything seemed to catch fire!

Mount Everest was only about 100 kilometers away, and we could see it on clear days. I still treasure the autograph of Tenzing Norgay, the first man to conquer the world's loftiest peak.

An Exquisite, But Confusing Land

I remember another train journey to boarding school a few years later. This time our train traveled south, and my travelling companion was my younger sister, Jennifer. We embarked again at Howrah Railway Station in Calcutta to journey to Madras, India's fourth-largest city. Madras, now called Chennai, is located on the Bay of Bengal and is the capital of the state of Tamil Nadu.

The Indian Railway has suffered tremendous deterioration and decay, but in those days Howrah Station still held much of the grandeur that had made it one of the greatest imperial achievements of the British Raj. I will probably never again experience the unique railway travel that India once offered.

Energetic Indian porters in their bright red jackets scrambled toward us as prospective clients, ferociously competing for our business. They proudly displayed the polished brass license tags that indicated they were legal baggage carriers. They veered us away from the illegitimate scoundrels who masqueraded as porters with the intention of stealing our luggage.

We hired some sinewy carriers and watched them lift our unwieldy school trunks without effort. With luggage precariously balanced high on their heads, they scurried through the teeming multitudes. Millions of people travel daily by train throughout India.

My sister and I struggled to keep up with our porters. We pushed and shoved our way through maimed beggars in filthy rags who clawed at us desperately, moaning for money, brushing them aside disdainfully. Hand in hand we tried to find our way through hundreds of panicky second-and third-class passengers seeking unoccupied seats in overcrowded coaches.

Things weren't made any easier by the sanctified cows, which were given free domain along the station platforms. We ducked and swerved past farmers clutching a variety of animals, all going to market at the end of their own train ride.

At last, with sighs of relief, we arrived at our first-class, air-conditioned compartment. We were met by a smartly dressed guard who led us to our reserved sleeping car. He opened the door to reveal a spotless cabin with freshly starched sheets neatly fitting

Caryl and her little sister

the bunk beds. Everything was tailored to perfection. Our luggage was heaved into the sleeper, and we settled down for a long journey.

Butlers in crisp, white uniforms whisked efficiently along the corridors with food and beverage orders. The stationmaster's whistle blew. The heavy, hissing steam engine responded. We were off.

Throughout the night we stopped at various stations. I woke to familiar sounds in the background. More passengers fought to get on the already overloaded train. There was occasional havoc when fights broke out between people, all claiming the same "reserved" seat. These occurred because bribes at the ticket office could miraculously duplicate reserved seat numbers.

Above the sounds of quarrels rose the shouts of vendors attempting to sell their wares up and down the platform. They tried to out yell each other: "Hot tea!" "Snacks!" "Fruits and nuts!" "Books, magazines, and papers!" "Shoeshine or shave!"

Occasionally a wandering beggar would startle me as he rapped sharply on our closed window, hoping to gain a tossed coin or two.

At Madras, we broke our journey. I clearly remember my first sight of the large and lovely beaches there. The beautiful old city traces its first European settlement back 500 years to the Portuguese.

Jennifer and I toured the seventeenth-century Fort Saint George, which overlooks the sparkling waters of the Bay of

Bengal. The oldest Anglican Church in India, Saint Mary's, is located there.

Spectacular Saint Thomas' Cathedral houses the traditional grave of Thomas the Apostle. He was the first Christian to bring the Gospel of Jesus Christ to India. Saint Thomas died a martyr in Madras, but not before establishing an enormous Christian community.

After our sightseeing tour, Jennifer and I freshened up a little. Then we boarded a smaller train to climb 7600 feet up the blue-green mountains to Ootacamund. The complete journey from Calcutta took us three days.

Because of the blistering-hot summer months in India, the British established hill stations or resort communities where their wives and children could escape the worst of the heat. "Ooty," our name for Ootacamund, is known as the Queen of Hill Resorts. With its cool woodlands and lake, it is one of the most popular summer retreats.

Our school walks took us through pine forests and flowers galore. Those were days of cool afternoons, astonishing panoramic vistas, and fresh eucalyptus air.

India is a rich, fertile land of endless agricultural potential. It is a scenically beautiful nation, too, a fact that eludes many Westerners. The sheltered environment of our boarding school provided us with hundreds of pleasant hours in the heart of India's countryside, seaside, and mountains.

But it is the people of India I remember best. I can still see the sober, efficient nuns from my school in Calcutta, with their stiffly starched habits sweeping behind them and their Rosary beads clicking ceaselessly along the convent corridors.

The mountain villages were filled with cheerful peasants. Laugh lines crinkled around merry brown eyes as they greeted me with polite friendliness.

The streets of the cities swarmed with beggars. And the beggars' expressions were all the same: they were living memorials to pain and hopelessness.

There were our beloved servants' faces in our home. There were sad-eyed children's faces along the sidewalks. There were shrewd merchants' faces in the shops and bazaars. And there were empty, vacant faces among the *holy men* or Yogis.

Our British colonial traditions and lifestyle surrounded me with romantic elitism. Prestigious private clubs—the Tollygunge and Royal Turf Clubs, with all their pomp and old splendor—exposed me to once-in-a-lifetime social experiences.

However, it was the extreme wealth of certain Indian friends that introduced me to an elegance I never could have encountered in European homes. Their palatial dwellings overflowed with antiques and fine art. Maharajs and upper-class Indians entertained British royalty and ambassadors with extravagant hospitality.

Elaborate weddings would last for days, sometimes weeks. They were replete with Brahmin ritual and offered the most mouth-watering vegetarian delicacies imaginable. These events gave me early insights into India's strange religious customs.

Despite all the glamour, there was a dark side of India that even my childish spirit could discern. It was in Calcutta that I first became aware of India's primary religion—Hinduism—and confronted it in all its raw, pagan confusion.

Mumbai (formerly Bombay), India

Religious temple in the Himalaya Mountains

Engraving of 1800s view of Calcutta

Three

Living in a Paradox

It was Sunday morning in Calcutta—4:15 a.m. to be exact. Our Indian servant rapped on the outside of our bedroom window. "Time to get up, Misy-baba! Time to get ready for church!"

Jennifer and I rubbed our eyes, dressed quickly and quietly, and let ourselves out the front door. "Shh. Don't wake up Mummy and Daddy," my sister whispered hoarsely. We left the house and long driveway behind us. Silently closing the compound gate, we waited on the sidewalk for our transportation.

It was a cold winter morning. I remember jumping up and down on my skinny legs trying to keep warm. I puffed the warm breath out of my mouth and held it against my cheeks and ears with my gloved, cupped hands. Jenny and I would take turns blowing hot air on each other's backs and laughing. We called our game "hot potatoes."

Every moment or two we would look anxiously down the road, straining our eyes to peer through the dense fog. Was the familiar outline of a car driving toward us yet? The thick cloud wasn't really moisture; it was mostly smoke billowing from thousands of cow-dung fires that had been burning throughout the night.

The smell of those fires lay in thick blankets on the cold morning air. It stung our eyes. At last we saw the car draw up through the grayness. The excitement of seeing our friends made us forget the cold, impatient wait. We jumped into the crammed car, chattering merrily all the way to Mass.

All God's Creatures Equal?

Our Roman Catholic church was awesome to me, standing out majestically against the dilapidated buildings surrounding it. Leaving the car, we elbowed our way through begging throngs and entered the lush sanctuary.

We searched for a place where all nine of us could sit together as we moved down the aisle. Usually we had to be separated, so I always watched for the cleanest, best-looking people to sit next to. Most of the worshipers were outcasts by orthodox Hindu standards—their mixed blood or low class relegating them to the most inferior social position.

After finding my seat, I began to absorb the beauty around me. Richly decorated statues stood in dozens of little alcoves along the walls. Marble floors gleamed. Enormous vases containing assorted freshly cut flowers were everywhere, their scent mingling with that of sweet, heavy incense.

Suddenly the organ began to play powerfully. The nuns burst into hymns as the priest arrived in his lavish apparel. He was followed by the clerical entourage with all its ornamental religious trimmings. This magnificent procession moved regally through the poor congregation.

In his message, the priest said that in God's eyes, all people are equal. Looking around, I knew we didn't really believe that. In India, how could we all be equal?

He said we should love our neighbors. Yet in the very process of leaving the church building, I knew we all would push aside the lepers and beggars who crowded against us. I would harshly scold them in my childish way if they so much as touched me.

I recall on one occasion opening my bulging purse. To whom would I give the shiny coins it held? Which leper was worst off?

Which beggar was in most need? I couldn't decide. Instead, I closed the purse and chose to ignore them all.

Driving home from church, we passed hundreds of icons—idols that are worshiped by the Indian people. Bowls of rice, flowers, and petals were strewn in front of these phallic-looking stones, which are placed on almost every street corner. Barren women kiss the stones in hopes of producing a male child. Sometimes they superstitiously smear the stone with red dye to make it look bloody. As a child this repulsed me, although I didn't know why.

Some of the trees that we passed had small altars of stones at their bases, surrounded by flowers and dye. Passersby would touch the altars, with the same hand touch their lips and their foreheads, then touch the stones again. At times I wondered—*why would anyone worship stones and trees?*

A common sight was that of a man worshiping a cow. A cow would be resting on the sidewalk. A man would cup his hands together, bringing them to his forehead. With a deeply respectful gesture, he would bow low. The cow invariably ignored this adoration.

One day I saw a cow possessively nursing her young calf on the crowded sidewalk. A passing man accidently nudged the young animal. With deep regret, the man bowed toward the mother. She responded by hotly kicking the poor fellow!

Every little shop and street vendor's cart we passed was cluttered with photos, paintings, or idols of fierce-looking gods. These deities were adorned with garlands of marigolds. Sticks of incense burned in front of them. Shiva, Vishnu, Kali, and Durga were the ones I immediately recognized because they were most frequently worshiped.

Some of the other gods had bodies of half-animals or trees. Others had faces of monkeys and elephants. And there was always the snake. Sometimes it was entwined around the gods. Sometimes it covered them in protection. It always made goose bumps run up my arms. It looked scary.

Kali stuck her tongue out, blood dripping everywhere. She wore dozens of skulls around her neck and stood on a blood-smeared corpse. All this frightened me. These gods looked so threatening! How, I asked myself, could people worship such terrifying deities?

My mind went back to our church. The statues there were so serene. All the saints that we worshiped seemed appealing and kind. I remember the hours I had spent looking into their gentle eyes and pleading with them to get me into the presence of God. They were the ones I believed had direct access to the Father.

I prayed to the Virgin Mary. I lit candles before Saint Theresa, whose name I took at my confirmation. I kneeled before Saint Joseph, the stepfather of Jesus. These and countless other lesser saints all helped, I believed, to further my good rapport with God.

I had been taught that the saints assured my progress through the afterlife—through Paradise and Purgatory. Eventually, with their help, I hoped to reach Heaven.

Salvation could be mine, I believed, if I prayed enough Stations of the Cross and Rosary circles. I needed to attend enough benedictions, Masses, and retreats. And I couldn't do too many bad things.

My regular visits to the priest for *confession* were just for *venial* (pardonable) sins. He would give me strings of prayers to offer for absolution. After repeating them, I would feel very good and proud of myself, until my sister and I got into another fight. This always seemed to happen too quickly. Then, all at once, I was a sinner again!

Still, in spite of these complexities, I felt that my religion was greatly superior to that of the Hindu. For one thing, his burden was far larger than mine because he had lives galore behind him and ahead of him to deal with. The notion of the Hindu's reincarnation was more complicated than my Catholic belief in one afterlife, even though I did get muddled with the uncertainties of Hell, Purgatory, and Heaven.

My deepest childhood wrestlings were not so much with dogma as with emotions. I was particularly affected at times like Christmas. To me, Christmas was a season of peace and goodwill, of social action and compassion. Yet our traditional celebrations reflected few of these values.

We would buy and make Christmas presents for close family

and dear friends. My parents would bring in extra food to feed specially invited Christmas Eve guests. Enormous, expensive Christmas baskets arrived during the days preceding December 25th, sent by Father's business acquaintances.

There was too much food and drink for our small household to consume, but at this happy time we didn't think of sharing with the poor communities around us. We were being "charitable" to our privileged, chosen friends. We busied ourselves with party preparations by decorating the house with Christmas ornaments. A huge Christmas tree was brought in. We adorned it with trimmings and topped it with the finishing touch, the Christmas tree fairy!

The night before Christmas Eve we had a family tradition that remains a very precious memory. Jennifer and I would bathe, get dressed up, and wait for Mum and Dad to return from the office. We would pile the car seats high with Christmas gifts, then climb in ourselves. With enthusiastic spirits we would set out to deliver packages to all our friends in different parts of the city. We would sing Christmas carols in the car, each one trying to out-sing the other. After all, wasn't this the season of happiness and good cheer?

Yet, in contrast, as we drove through the wretched streets, I saw no sign of Christmas blessing on the faces of the Indian people. The only reminder of Christmas was a tree here or there, blinking dimly in the darkness. The offices of an occasional

A potter in the streets of India

Christian business glowed quietly with sparse decorations. Scattered churches bore Christmas messages. But otherwise the overwhelming poverty remained untouched.

As usual, the public walkways were crowded with unsheltered sleeping bodies. Children curled up against each other like tiny rats, trying to keep warm in the cold winter night. *No Christmas presents for them*, I thought sadly. Small groups of men sat huddled around smoking cow-dung fires. *Do those smelly containers give out any warmth at all?* I wondered.

The Indian Caste System

I remember when some of my father's Hindu business friends asked us to stop by their home to join them for a Christmas party. We turned off the road and stopped before tall, closed iron gates. The security guard recognized my father and opened them. We drove up the winding entrance to a spacious house and parked. How different this was from the dismal shacks that lined the streets outside! Laughter, music, and happy conversation floated from the open veranda doors and across softly lit, lush, manicured lawns. Long, friendly shadows stretched toward us in welcome. It was all such a contrast to the squalid footpaths beyond the gates.

"These Indians must be very rich," I said with wonderment to my parents. When I asked them how well off they were, Mum and Dad both laughed. "This caste owns the banks and many large businesses."

Child that I was, I didn't understand that the Hindu sacred texts were responsible for one of the most strongly held religious principles in Indian consciousness—the caste system.

Castes are, in principle, determined by the color of one's skin. Lighter skin is supposed to reflect the purity of one's blood. Hindu scriptures teach that dark-skinned people can hope for salvation only by becoming lighter skinned in future incarnations. However, one is born into a caste, or category, and must remain in that status until death.

The highest caste, whose members are known as Brahmins,

or priests, are said to be the product of the god, Brahma—the Creator (a personification of Brahman, Hindu-reality and *god-consciousness*). Brahmins are on an equal level with Brahma's brain, and are revered as gods. They are destined to fulfill the high functions of spiritual priesthood and alone are able to lead their fellowmen to "salvation" through their prayers and rituals.

The Kshatryas, who hold political power, are believed to issue from Brahma's shoulders. They are therefore endowed with physical force, and are the kings and warriors.

The Vaisyas, or peasants, tradespeople, and farmers, are aligned with Brahma's belly. They provide food, clothing and other bodily necessities for man.

The Sudras, or serfs (mechanics, craftsmen, laborers, or mere servants) come from his feet and are considered servants of the first three castes.

The Untouchables form the last and lowest group of Indian society. They are people of no caste–so far beneath the Sudras that they are outside the social order. They perform the most menial jobs such as laundering clothes, street sweeping, butchering animals, handling cadavers, cleaning sewers or latrines, and so on. Their work and non-status are thought to make them impure, and their impurity can contaminate the higher castes. Thus, they were not to touch or even come anywhere near members of the first three castes. The Untouchables were renamed Harajans by Ghandi and are today called Dalit.

To the Untouchables are added the pariahs, or outcasts, people expelled from the castes into which they were born for social or religious sins.

Although caste discrimination has been officially outlawed, it is still firmly entrenched in Indian culture. Millions of Indians are victims of a system of racism and oppression that defies any comparison worldwide.

Karma, the Hindu law of cause-and-effect, determines a person's caste in his present lifetime. Reincarnation supposedly continues a soul's progress (or regression) through the various castes.

Like most Westerners in India, our family had servants to maintain our household. However, unlike Indian families, we had servants from many different subcastes and religions. This is frowned upon by Orthodox Hindus, who believe that only those of the same caste as themselves can work in their homes.

I remember wondering why the servant who did all our menial cleaning, sweeping, and scrubbing was always being verbally abused. His head and eyes were continually downcast. Often he crawled around the house on all fours like an animal.

One day, I rounded a corner in time to see one of the other servants kick him. He made no objection, but just received the blow in silence. I don't think I ever saw the man laugh or have a conversation with the other servants. He simply took their orders and bore their discipline. He never ate with them. Eventually I learned that he was an untouchable. He was consequently treated as if he were subhuman.

The daughters of our Roman Catholic chauffeur were the same ages as Jenny and I. We were told never to enter the servants' quarters, but one day we ignored the restrictions. With trepidation, we ventured to the bottom of our compound where the workers lived.

Our servants considered themselves privileged workers. They had a room for each family, plus a communal bathtub and flushing toilet. In comparison to the majority of the population of India, I can see why they counted their blessings. However, I was shocked when I came to the single room that harbored our driver, his wife, and his two children.

It took only a few seconds for me to realize that this room, which acted as their living room, bedroom, and dining room, was smaller than the bathroom that my sister and I shared!

Jenny and I walked meekly into the dark room, dimly lit by only one tiny barred window. I don't suppose that room had ever seen the sun. In my shame, I excused that fact, rationalizing that at least the room was cool.

We asked the girls' mother if they could come and play with us in our house. She covered her head, nose, and mouth with her sari before speaking to us. Eyes down, she said, "They cannot go into your house. You may play with them outside if you wish."

At first I wondered why the girls couldn't come and sleep overnight with us in our bedroom like our other friends. Before long I was informed they were considered beneath us. Even though they were Roman Catholics like we were, and they attended our church, because they were servants we couldn't get too familiar with them.

So, while Jenny and I played with dolls dressed in brighter clothes than they wore, the girls played with sticks and mud. While we slept in soft beds, they slept on the floor of their tiny room on thin mats.

The Paradox of Animals

As the years went by, I gradually grew hardened and felt superior. Eventually, I accepted my role in the structure of society as one who was privileged and "above" certain other people.

But as a child, I remember thinking that our dog had it better than our next-door neighbors, let alone the millions of people who filled the streets of Calcutta. Sandy was a beautiful golden retriever and my faithful friend. Every day our sweeper boy, the outcast servant I mentioned earlier, brushed her and took her for a walk. The portion of food he fed her daily was probably more than he ate biweekly. It was certainly more nutritious. Sandy was allowed the run of the house, which gave her more freedom than any of the servants. And Sandy was allowed to sleep on our soft beds, while they slept on cold, mud floors.

If the people of India led more difficult lives than Sandy, the dogs of India bore little or no resemblance to her proud canine heritage.

The animals I saw as a child in India were pathetic sights—emaciated skeletons that freely roamed the streets. Although considered to be sacred, many animals were treated with tragic cruelty.

Mongrel dogs came in all shapes and sizes and were covered with sores, boils, and diseases. Rabies was rampant.

One Saturday morning I watched in horror as a car deliberately ran onto the back of a dog. The front of the car knocked the dog down. The rear ran over half the animal. The occupants of the car drove off honking their horn gleefully. The dog lay screaming in agony. No one even acknowledged the crazed animal as it lay bleeding and dying. I can still hear the shrill cries.

The paradox of animals is unexplainable. I once saw a woman pulling two dead rats along on a string. "Why is she doing that, Mum?"

"Don't know, Caryl. Strange, isn't it? Maybe they're some sort of good-luck charm."

Down the road was a rat temple. There rats were worshiped as gods. The sacred story goes that a god returned as a rat in one of his reincarnations. After that, bowls of fresh milk were put out daily for the thousands of rats in the crawling, infested temple. Milk, too expensive for the peasants to afford regularly for themselves, was fed to the rats every day. Meanwhile, the rats would bite, spread disease, and ultimately kill. Yet Hindus were forbidden to destroy them.

In Hinduism it is believed that if you destroy an animal, you may return as that animal in your next reincarnation. Yet, absurdly, cruelty toward animals continues.

Consider the cow. The cow is vital to Indian life—so vital, in fact, that some people say that in order to preserve the cow in a land that has no regard for life, cattle had to be made sacred. The cow is worshiped as a god and believed to be a reincarnation of an Indian deity.

In a more practical sense, its conservation is essential to provide milk, to use as a beast of burden, and to supply dung.

Cow-dung is used to build homes. Mixed with straw and mud, it forms the walls of the poor man's humble abode. It is used as fuel for fires. It is used as a cosmetic. Many times I have seen it matted into children's hair as a bleaching agent. It serves as a sort of poor man's henna. Cow urine is caught and drunk as a sacred ritual by the holy men of India.

Yet in spite of being sacred, even the cow does not escape without some peculiar abuses. I often saw the tiny carcass of a calf tied around a bamboo pole with a piece of dirty string. The cow would rub her head up and down against the contraption, almost as if to reassure herself that her calf was still alive. Why? The superstitious owner believed that while the mother could smell and see her baby, she would continue to give milk. So the smelly carcass, covered with flies, would accompany the milkman and his cow door-to-door as he delivered milk.

If superstition led to cruelty, so did money. One day I saw a little beggar boy who could not have been more than six years old. On his back was strapped a stiff, tiny baby. The baby's head lolled to one side, both little arms hung limply to its sides, and one tiny hand rigidly clutched a hard piece of bread. The beggar boy knew he could solicit funds more easily while his baby sister hung from his back. I watched her lifeless body, then looked into her brother's knowing eyes and examined his crooked half-smile. Was she really dead? How long had he been carting her little frame around for financial gain?

What bewilderment I felt as a little girl, observing the inhumane culture that paralyzed India! But my heart hardened to the sight of suffering early. It was, in one sense, a mercy. Callousness is almost necessary for emotional survival in that strange land.

As I grew up, superficial religious contrasts and similarities between my own religion, at the time Roman Catholicism, and the religion of India, intrigued me. The caste system perplexed me. Unkindness to human and animal alike troubled me. But beneath it all was something more frightening, more chilling than these outward manifestations.

For within the heart of Hinduism lies something troubling. The core of this religion claims reality to be an illusion known as Maya. In the months and years to come, I would be confronted with Hinduism's strange view of the world again and again. And the more I saw, the less I understood.

The streets of an Indian town

A *sacred* cow meanders through a market,
chewing its cud in Delhi India

Four

Milestones in Madness

I had enjoyed my usual midday nap on that warm Calcutta afternoon. Now I was bathed and dressed for a late-day stroll with my nanny. Hand in hand we walked down our short cul-de-sac toward the main road. Our destination was the shabby little park not far away from our compound.

Suddenly a growling half-man, half-animal like creature came careening toward us. He ran along the filthy gutter beside the sidewalk, groveling in the pungent refuse and grunting madly. His almost-naked body was caked in dirt and excrement. He didn't seem to see us at first. I was terrified and clung tightly to my startled companion.

Abruptly he looked up. I will never forget the encounter I had with the sheer madness in his eyes. His wild face was encircled with an explosion of filthy matted hair.

I screamed. He violently jumped on me. Clawing, gyrating madly with his hindquarters like an animal in heat, he grasped my body, pulsating against me.

With blind courage my nanny kicked the creature as though he were a mad dog, and much like a crazed beast, he began yelping and cowering. He ran off into the gutter and on his way.

This character was just one of thousands of Shivites, recognizable by the three horizontal lines painted on his forehead. These disciples of the god Shiva consider madness, one of Shiva's attributes, to be one of the highest levels of spirituality! Many Hindus believe insanity to be a form of god-consciousness.

Sadhus, holy men, and ascetics are sometimes reverently called *pagal*. This simply means insane. Ramakrishna, spiritual leader of many Westerners, once said, "The true saint behaves as though he were mad."

Sacred Madmen

Many years after my encounter with the crazed Shivite, I asked a knowledgeable Hindu why these ferocious madmen and women are allowed to inhabit the streets. Why were they free to attack whomever they randomly chose?

"Madmen, no matter how fearsome," he replied condescendingly, "must be reverenced. They have sacred privileges. They are divine!"

He went on to explain that these people could communicate with the spirit world. Their supposed encumbrances are just symbolic messages with hidden meanings. Their apparent mental displacement is really a higher state of consciousness!

Altered states of consciousness are an integral part of Hindu god-consciousness. A self-induced hypnotic trance, a drugged mind, or possession by a spirit are all features of Hindu religiosity. These activities are not only found among serious holy men but are common among many typical Indian people.

As a matter of fact, during certain religious holidays, the public at large seems to go entirely berserk. One such occasion is Holi, The Festival of Colors. Holi is considered part of the harvest festival. Its roots lie in fertility rites. The sprinkling of lavish amounts of red dye everywhere represents the female menses.

Because of its symbolism, Holi is a time when Indian women are free to loosen up their behavior. They can flirt to their heart's content. They can choose their own mates. They can even wield a stick at whatever man catches their fancy.

Today, as during my childhood, and for centuries past, Holi begins with the last full moon in March. It is believed that at this time Mother Earth awakens after her long winter paralysis. Although known as the Harvest Festival, Holi is more widely associated with the legend of Krishna.

Krishna (the god of the familiar Hare Krishna) is known as a mischievous thief and flirt. He was the god who, in legend, had a passion for stealing butter and the clothes of the village maidens while they bathed in the nearby pond.

The villages where Krishna and his divine love, Radha the milkmaid, are supposed to have lived celebrate a unique form of Holi. Everyone, from young children to sober old women,

Elephant on the streets of a city in India, during Holi—
this elephant is painted in bright shades of red.

partakes of *bhang*, a kind of hashish. Bhang is made from hemp. It is mixed in *thandai*, a cold drink consisting of milk, nuts, and clotted cream. This concoction is considered particularly appropriate for Holi's festivities.

After much singing, dancing, and bhang, the madness of Holi really begins. Anyone foolish enough to be out in the streets is showered with dye of every hue. Colors fill the air—clouds of magenta, yellow, green, and crimson cover people from head to toe.

The streets vibrate with mischief and laughter. Little boys hide on buildings and behind walls to surprise unsuspecting passersby. Everything imaginable is used to squirt people. Containers ranging from old bicycle pumps to discarded spray cans are filled with a mixture of dye and water. For weeks after Holi, people still wear this holiday décor in their hair and clothing.

This mayhem persists into the night. When darkness falls, sounds of worship can be heard from surrounding temples. Brahmin priests collect money. Vendors peddle countless flowers and petals, plus enormous amounts of blood-red dye. Worshipers throw colored powder over the temple floors. They boldly tint their tinseled deities.

By then, everyone is high on bhang. Women, intoxicated and uninhibited, dance with inviting smiles and twisted saris. Each female somehow believes

Growing up in India—
intriguing yet often frightening

that she is Radha, Krishna's sweetheart, dancing for her lord. Musicians sway to the sounds of their instruments. Amplified noise is everywhere. Only the animals in the streets are unmoved by all the chaos, though even they unwittingly participate—dye covering stray dog and sacred cow alike.

I vividly remember the madness and chaos of different festivals I saw as a child. The drug-induced devotees frightened me. Loud, hypnotic, repetitive music kept me awake many a night.

Bittersweet Departure

The years my sister and I spent in boarding school took us to different areas of India. This exposed us to varying religious festivals, as well as new gods and goddesses. The separation from our parents that schooling imposed taught us a unique independence. When we were older, we were sent to boarding school in England, and we saw our parents only once every two years. At age seventeen, I returned to India to attend college.

By my nineteenth year however, insanity and instability was gripping India. Politically, the situation was growing more and more dangerous. Three factors made it increasingly difficult to maintain a calm existence. One was Communist agitation. Another was the swelling population. As a result of Calcutta's industrial growth, millions of unemployed farmers were taking jobs in the cities. The resulting friction and overcrowding made life almost unbearable. The third factor was a recent war with Pakistan.

That war's violence was still a fresh memory for our family that disturbing year. Tight curfews had been enforced daily, making normal life impossible. City streets had been out-of-bounds; minor brawls and major battles had filled the night with the noise of gunfire. Sirens suddenly sounded as aircraft thundered across the skies. We knew that heavy bombing was killing multitudes at the India-Pakistan border, just a few miles away.

Countless refugees had escaped and flooded the already over-populated city. Calcutta simply couldn't cope with the additional strain. Disease, polluted drinking water, food shortages, power and energy blackouts—all contributed to utter confusion.

As a family, we experienced the additional horror of having a dangerous mob surround our home. Several months of political and labor disputes had affected the factories that my father managed. Angry strikers, incited by Communist agitators, decided to take the law into their own hands. Their intention was to pressure the management. If it meant killing them for "the cause," then they would. My father and other Europeans were expected to give in to their financial demands.

One morning the screaming crowd arrived. For hours we were barricaded in our compound, encircled by raging throngs. Overexcited and drug-crazed, these thousands of protesters were completely out of control. The police refused to help us. They said their interference would be too dangerous. "To whom?" I wondered. "Us or them?"

My father made a desperate decision. All the servants had fled. Only our faithful Roman Catholic driver stood by our side. We

Map of India and the surrounding world

climbed into the car and drove through the savage crowd without police escort. Our only alternative was to wait for our house to be mobbed or burned down. Either way we would probably have been killed.

Slowly, slowly our big sedan pushed its way through thronging masses. Strangers shouted and screamed obscenities at us. They pressed their frothy mouths against the car windows. They pounded their fists on the roof and beat on the sides of the car. Desperately they tried to break their way in through the locked doors to drag us out.

By some miracle we were spared. Others were not so fortunate. Some of my father's business associates were badly beaten. This turn of events caused Father to consider leaving India earlier than anticipated. After all our years there, it was a heart-wrenching conclusion. How could we leave everyone behind?

When it was safe to return to our house, we wondered how we could ever get everything moved! My sister and I looked around with nostalgia. Our house was decorated in typical colonial style: wicker furniture on a veranda framed by large open arches to catch evening breezes; marble floors to cool the house during summer, peppered with heavily embossed Indian carpets.

Caryl and her family

Memories were stored in almost every corner. Although I hadn't spent my infant years there, I had lived the last sixteen, on and off, under this roof. Our departure wasn't going to be easy.

Soon, however, the house was piled high with packing boxes. Furniture was crated. Carpets were rolled and insulated for the long sea voyage ahead. Our clothes were mothballed in heavy chests for the six-month journey. My heart sank to discover that old, favorite possessions had to be left behind. Nevertheless, we were going, and life for me would take on a whole new meaning.

Five

Landing in the Butter

London swings like a pendulum do,
And I swung with the momentum too—
Jet-setting, fast life, to mention a few
Of the new trends that led my life askew.
Addiction to excitement led me forward, led me on;
Each *high* led to needs that were too deep to drown.
My search through alternatives, bizarre and unknown,
In the end got me lost, confused, and alone.[1]

A New Beginning

The springtime freshness of England seemed to welcome us. Driving through the city to the train station, we were comforted by the golden greetings of 10,000 sunlit daffodils. Crocuses and snowdrops popped their heads through the spring-green grass. Budding trees promised a glorious summer. What a difference between the two countries! The English streets seemed empty by comparison to the teeming Indian sidewalks on which thousands lived and died. The tidiness and cleanliness of English surroundings was a welcome sight. People actually followed traffic rules. No cows roamed freely causing endless traffic jams.

The train ride to our new home on the south coast of England was a sunny, exciting journey. With growing hope, we shared new plans.

Our home-to-be was my mother's inheritance, left to her by my grandfather many years before. On the other side of the world we had schemed and designed its new look for months. Now here we were at last, able to put our ideas to work. Busy weeks of shopping in the chaos of Indian bazaars were paying off. Soon our new abode looked like something from a cover story of an interior design magazine. The knickknacks from India soothed our aching hearts.

Spring turned into summer, and a hot one at that. By its end I was beginning to become disenchanted with country living. My part-time job was unfulfilling. I dreamed of a career in London. That elegant old city captured my imagination. I was feeling restless. The sparseness of people in our little village made life seem dull, boring, monotonous. I wasn't used to living in a suburban home. I wasn't used to life with parents. *I need freedom*, I thought. For me, it was time to move on.

Not sure what kind of job I wanted, I searched the London newspapers for work. I was amazed to find myself hired for the first job I applied for. It was in an art studio, designing tapestries for the wealthy and aristocratic. I was overwhelmed!

Maggy, my best school friend, and I managed to discover a cheap little apartment in a rather seedy part of West London. We were blind to its ugliness and drawbacks; we only saw its great potential. The two of us puffed and panted as we hauled our meager possessions up five flights of dirty stairs to the poky attic accommodations we considered "our penthouse suite."

Before long, new friends introduced us to the trends and temptations of swinging London. I choked as I attempted to enjoy my first puffs of cigarette smoke. I struggled to overcome the horrendous effects of alcoholic hangovers. Parties, drugs, and promiscuity offered a panorama of enticements.

I was emerging from a stiff and restricting cocoon. Suddenly life was beautiful. Freedom was intoxicating. I bravely stretched my new wings and began to fly.

"Caryl Frances, you were born with a silver spoon in your mouth. You are just downright lucky!" said my mum with an affectionate laugh. She passed me another hot buttered crumpet, which I devoured hungrily with my freshly poured tea. I had traveled to my parents' Hampshire home for the weekend to share my exciting news.

"Well, go on," coaxed my father, "tell us more." I rattled on with impassioned enthusiasm describing a new opportunity. Several weeks earlier I had seen an advertisement in a London newspaper for an artist to work on television projects for the British Broadcasting Company.

What nerve I have, I had thought, climbing the stairs to the interview. *Imagine me applying to work with the famous BBC. Well, anything is worth a try. All they can say is, "No, sorry, you're no good."*

"Have another crumpet, or some cake," tempted my mum.

"Oooh, yes please!" I replied quickly, then checked myself. Almost too deliberately and slowly, I helped myself to more. I didn't want my parents to notice my ravenous snatchings.

"Don't you ever feed yourself in London?" asked my dad. "You almost eat us out of house and home on these weekend visits of yours!"

Little did he know how close to the truth he had come. I invariably filled my stomach well with mum's home cooking, and more likely than not it kept me going through the whole week. But I didn't want to worry them with my financial problems. In their eyes the only alternative would have been for me to move home again. I couldn't do that—not now, not having tasted the glamour, excitement, and fast life of London.

As a result of my independent spirit, however, for months I had barely existed. My tapestry-designing job's meager salary had just about covered my low rent and other necessary expenses. It left me nothing for food or travel. I had taken an evening job at a bar to bring in some extra cash, but in return I had to sacrifice sleep.

A British Caste System

It was after months of living this way and becoming more and more physically run-down that I had spotted the challenging advertisement for an artist. Unable to afford a phone call for an appointment or the bus fare to travel across London for the interview, I had risked borrowing some money from my piggy bank. These funds were normally set aside each week for various bills. Nevertheless, I had taken a deep breath and gambled. And I had won! I was called back for several more interviews, and eventually the hoped-for acceptance came: "You've been chosen for the post. Can you start Monday?"

"Congratulations!" said Dad with encouraging gusto. He came over and kissed me warmly on the forehead. "Well done, woman." (his affectionate title for the women of his household). "I am proud of you."

The new job brought some much-needed extra income, and eventually enabled me to relocate in a more exclusive London area. My flatmates and I made several subsequent moves, each time to a nicer apartment. We were able to afford more nourishing meals. Our upwardly mobile lifestyle led us to new, more exciting friends.

I was deluged with invitations from young men. For sheer self-gratification, I focused on those whom I felt would offer the most interesting, stimulating company.

One of my beaus was a Cambridge University undergraduate. Because of him I was able to enjoy an aspect of British social life I had never before experienced. The wondrous, frivolous summer that he and I shared is among my most nostalgic remembrances.

I relished hours of boating on waterways that ran behind the colleges. There were champagne breakfast parties and evening cocktail occasions on the perfectly manicured lawns of the prestigious colleges. It was a thrill to mingle with "high society"—to attend balls, where dancing to orchestras, rock and roll groups, and Jamaican tin bands continued until the early hours of the morning. I felt like Cinderella and Alice in Wonderland. I wondered if my bubble would ever burst.

For the time, it didn't. Instead, life's journey grew more and more adventurous. I embarked on new, unimagined escapades, many of which seemed very different from the way of life I had experienced in India. In retrospect, I can see there were similarities, particularly when it came to hobnobbing with the social elite.

I gradually developed a socially arrogant attitude, which drew me with a magnetic seduction into snobbish circles. I developed a sense of superiority and attached great importance to various airs and graces. It became my habit to look down on those who came from a different "class."

In England it is quite easy to determine who has had a private education and who has come from middle to upper-middle-class social backgrounds. It didn't take me long to begin putting people into social categories. To which clubs did they belong? Where did they dine? What fashionable trends did they follow? In what area did they live?

Wasn't this kind of value judgment similar to the attitudes that the caste system created in India? I was reflecting a practice I had abhorred as a child. Yet now I was justifying it as an established part of British etiquette.

At the time, my whirlwind social madness prevented me from pondering such deep, ethical questions. Instead I continued, with relish, to pursue the foolishness of youth.

A romantic Frenchman introduced me to the sparkling gambling casinos and posh nightlife of London. Soon this absorbed my early-morning hours too. My childhood friends who were returning from India invited me to visit them at their chic country homes for weekends. Some of them got married in grandiose hotels and private clubs in London. I remember attending some of those spectacular events with an air of disbelieving amazement. Surely all this existed only in storybooks and dreams.

In one particularly vivid recollection, I can still see myself tripping lightly down, one of the main streets in the West End of London. I was filled with the bubbles of expensive champagne, dizzy with intoxication and excitement. I had just attended a lavish wedding at London's celebrated Ritz Hotel. The day had deepened into a crisp, sunny autumn evening. Clear blue skies and lengthening shadows embraced the city. I had a dear boyfriend on one arm and London all around me. *Ah. What a life!*

Over the ensuing months, my fast-paced social life continued to take me to all sorts of glamorous and exciting events. I was privileged to meet the famous from all walks of life. I attended opening galas as well as theater and film premieres. I sat through exciting tennis championships in specially reserved seats at the prestigious Wimbledon Club. I went to the private pits at car-racing events, to the private boxes at horse races, and to the opera at the famous Glyndebourne Estate in Sussex.

My playing field extended beyond London, too. I traveled luxuriously throughout Europe. Winters

One of the beautiful old buildings in Piccadilly

were spent skiing in Austria, Switzerland, Germany, and Italy. Summers brought weeks of relaxation on the beaches of the Greek Islands, Spain, Portugal, and the notorious and exclusive French Riviera during the Cannes Film Festival.

All this made me greedy for more; I was on the fastest of carousels and didn't want to get off. "Life" meant fun and laughter, no commitments, no restrictions, no responsibilities, and a lot of freedom. Finally, when my job seemed too confining, I gave my notice.

Now I had complete liberty to travel around Europe. Two friends and I filled all the available space in our newly acquired sports car with holiday trappings. We hopped in, and for three months journeyed from England and through eleven countries. We drove the highways and byways of Europe. We stopped whenever the fancy took us, visiting local attractions and points of interest until we were walking encyclopedias. Our trip concluded with the Greek Isles in the beautiful Mediterranean.

Into the World of Art and Film

Despite our live-for-today philosophy, eventually tomorrow came. Upon returning home, I discovered with dismay that my bank accounts were almost empty. With no job to return to and an impassioned addiction to my accustomed expensive lifestyle and freedom, I ventured into the world of freelance art.

Driving ambition, stubborn tenacity, and pride kept me moving forward. Before long, open doors, introductions to the right people, and being at the right place at the right time brought about a successful business. At first I was on my own. Then I joined forces with a dear friend, Paul, and we established a financially viable art studio. Together we provided a wide spectrum of creative skills. Our efforts included graphic design and illustrating children's books, greeting cards, and wrapping paper. We also designed film titles and credits for two major movie studios, Shepperton and Pinewood.

Paul and I also pioneered touristy paraphernalia and gimmickry to promote "Swinging London," which by this time was earning quite a reputation worldwide. We were the interior designers of well-known nightclubs and restaurants. We developed logos and miscellaneous promotional material for theater projects, films, restaurants, clubs, and businesses.

I tried my hand at being the production coordinator for a film company. This entailed working on a series of TV commercials, and I thoroughly enjoyed the challenge and hard work. That assignment led to production work on various other film projects. Then came the chance to audition as an extra for a major movie called *A Clockwork Orange*. That role led to other small parts in other films.

This was an exciting step up the ladder for me, and it seemed like a happy progression. I had been involved in drama classes at school, and had done some modeling, even while growing up in India. In fact, it was really in India that I had been "discovered." I had been working in the art department of a well-known advertising agency in Calcutta. One day some art directors walked through our large studio, gloomily discussing a big, difficult advertising campaign. It seemed that in all their auditioning, they had not

London, with a view of the House of Parliament

come up with the right model to promote the product. Somehow, in the panic of the situation they looked over to my desk. The decision was made almost immediately: I was to be "the girl."

Soon full-page advertisements carrying my image had appeared in the big daily newspapers all over India. Enormous billboards in the big cities had me labeled "The Secretary of the Year." The promotional slogans of the campaign explained that I recommended a particular brand of typewriter. Fashion and trade magazines carried my picture. Soon people stopped me in the street for my autograph. I was only eighteen years old at the time and had never set my fingers on a typewriter keyboard!

Now in England, two years later, my modeling, film work, and artwork had led me to real success—more than I could ever have imagined. I had everything I desired in order to be financially content. By this time we lived in a super apartment in pretentious Chelsea, on *the* King's Road. We were in the heart of London's swinging jet-setters.

A series of exotic sports cars passed through my possession. I bought and sold several London properties, making a substantial profit on each sale. My wardrobe was nothing to scoff at. Only the best restaurants, nightclubs, and discos attracted me. I was becoming spoiled—about that there was no doubt. My mother's words would echo again and again in my mind. If it wasn't "You have a silver spoon in your mouth!" it was "Caryl Frances, you always land with your bottom in the butter!"

Life was very good to me. Yet I also recall an increasing frequency of deep, inner pain. I remember days of depression. I can still feel the loneliness and the struggle.

What was happening? I had every material thing I wanted and achieved all the success I could ask for. Yet I felt emotionally bankrupt.

My friendship with Paul had required an exceptional amount of effort and energy. Not surprisingly, with all the nurturing, it had blossomed into a special romance. We were two young, headstrong teenagers when we met. By the time we were in our early twenties, we had reached a level of success beyond our wildest expectations. Together we had overcome both professional and emotional obstacles.

In a moment of wild impulse, we decided to get married. We were soon swept along in the tide of social etiquette normally following such life-deciding announcements. Without seriously considering the ramifications of marital commitment, we followed the flow and became man and wife.

Within weeks our friendship began to sour. Our personalities began to violently clash, and our work relationship deteriorated beyond all feasibility. Angrily we separated. I knew that it takes two to build or break a partnership, and I had to concede that at least fifty percent of the aggravation was my fault. With shame, I came to realize that although in most areas I could accomplish nearly anything I set my mind to, in the emotional realm I was not so competent. My failure was not only a personal disgrace; I knew it reflected on my family as well. For that I felt particularly guilty.

The whole episode was horribly draining. Frustrated, I reached the point where I had to concede that I had no more inner resources. Only one solution made sense to me: I packed my bags with a few belongings, gathered a little money, and flew to another country. I would escape and lick my wounds. I would make a fresh start.

Six

In Search of the Lost Chord

The Bahama Islands seemed almost as far from reality as they were from Paul. Stunningly beautiful sunrises and sunsets provided the backdrops of each day. I would try to remember the details of every cloud formation and color combination and wondered if I would ever spot the same celestial painting twice. It never happened.

Clear, clean waters revealed sparkling coral reefs. Slender palm trees swayed in the unceasing ocean breezes and edged the brilliant turquoise sea. Here was beauty I had never before experienced. And it was so tranquil. The sound of ocean waves kissing miles of deserted white-sand beaches provided daily music. Night had its own enchantment, filled with the same music played somehow more peacefully. Its jet-black skies were uncluttered by human structures. There were no city lights, no silhouettes of steel and mortar skylines, only stars: thousands and thousands of them—indeed millions of stars—all shining, seemingly close.

Sometimes I would lie on the beach and look up at them. Sometimes I would stretch my hands up, feeling as if I could grasp them with my fingertips as night breezes whispered beneath the moonlight. The smell of the salt air seemed always so clean, so unpolluted. It was magnificent.

And once again, I had "landed with my bottom in the butter," for I had been invited to be part of a team that was to launch a promotional campaign to sell oceanfront parcels on this tiny island, Norman's Cay. My work involved creating and illustrating advertising material and following through with promotional publicity. I also helped with the interior design of the tiny restaurant and four little beach shacks that served as accommodations for prospective land buyers.

Over the weeks we organized recreational activities to keep our visitors amused. Tennis courts were built. We brought over a couple of beach jeeps from the mainland, and a dozen bicycles. We enjoyed speedboat trips around the island and discovered secluded beaches and coves. Scuba diving gear and snorkeling equipment allowed us to investigate the hidden beauties of the surrounding waters.

As publicity spread to the American mainland, an abundance of potential clients appeared. Their intention was to purchase plots and build summer homes. I had great fun dreaming with them, designing their homes, sharing their architects' plans, and painting my imagined rendition for them.

A Psychedelic World

During those weeks, I became bronzed by the sun and quieted by nature's soothing beauties. But a broken heart and disjointed emotions brought me back again and again to the reality of my emotional inadequacies. The pace of life was slow, allowing me much time by myself—perhaps too much time—to reflect and ponder. During those days of relaxed lifestyle and deep contemplation some visitors came to the island who introduced me to the intriguing world of drugs. I began by only sampling hashish and marijuana, but before long they became my daily habits.

My first exposure to drugs had actually taken place some months earlier in London. I had become increasingly dissatisfied with the social whirl there. Perhaps I had been looking for an alternative.

One spring afternoon, in a burst of energy I had suddenly decided to visit some friends down Kings Road in Chelsea. I arrived at their house and barged in enthusiastically. Entering the strangely quiet dining room, I encountered several hippies deeply engrossed in reflective silence. The room was filled with a pungent sweet smell and a blue-gray mist that gently stung my eyes. It seemed as though I had walked into a room where time and actions were caught in slow motion. It was like being in a vacuum, a deadness.

For fear of breaking the strangely reverent quiet, I found myself obeying a command to sit down. The eyes of some looked up and seemed to focus but not see me. Others ignored me, far too engrossed in some other world. I settled down, not quite knowing what to do or say. I soon realized that no one cared whether I did or said anything.

How strange, I thought. *This is quite different from the social etiquette I'm used to. My other friends always acknowledge everyone who comes into the room, and they always introduce themselves.* I was somewhat amused by the neglect of common courtesy.

The only movement in the unnatural stillness was the passing around the table of "the joint." It was a large, clumsy, hand-rolled marijuana cigarette. Four cigarette papers had been needed to roll this one, and strange, grassy-looking stuff hung out from the unlit end. Each member inhaled deeply from the joint and while passing it on, coughed and spluttered with great control so as little as possible of the hallucinogenic smoke escaped his lungs. I watched with intrigue. Each person had apparently mastered the technique of absorbing the most he could of the puff. Then, as the inhaled smoke was savored and, I assumed, had penetrated the bloodstream, each one nodded with appreciation and leaned back to acknowledge some amazing revelation taking place in his mind.

Suddenly the silence was broken. One fellow laughed loudly and abruptly. I was surprised because no one had said anything funny. What was he laughing at? Then someone else, as though hearing the same unspoken joke, started tittering too, and then another. I couldn't help but be perplexed at the madness of it all. I felt as though I had been admitted to some sort of bizarre insane asylum.

Suddenly, I found the joint had made its way to me. My friend nudged me to take it. Inwardly I panicked; I felt a chill of fear. I was terrified to inhale the smoke. I imagined losing control, like one of those strange, laughing space-cadets.

My predicament was apparent: I had interrupted the peaceful flow. The precious joint was burning down fast. Their eyes seemed to watch me accusingly. I felt embarrassed and didn't want anyone to know that all this was unfamiliar to me.

So, yielding to peer pressure and panic, I mimicked what I had seen the others do, and immediately understood why they had choked. The stuff burnt. It felt as though a hot, dry coal had stuck to my throat. I felt my eyes burn and tears roll down my cheeks. *Oh, how ghastly!* I winced as I passed the lethal object to the fellow on my right.

I sat waiting for something to happen, but nothing did—no hallucinations, no dizziness, no insanity. My throat didn't even cool down. The sensation was terrible, not at all what I had imagined. This couldn't have been what they had sung about so joyfully in the musical *Hair*, which I had seen only a few days before.

That *non* experience shattered my dreams. I was disappointed and confused by my failure and angry that I might have lost the chance forever to be part of the subculture that so intrigued me. At that point, I left the house and returned to the streets of London, where I felt a sense of mastery. I weighed my feelings of frustration and concluded, *I don't really want to be like those down-and-outs, anyway. Look what they've become.* To my way of thinking, they had lost their motivation and grown apathetic. They had somehow willfully submitted to their plight. Their strange inertia had reminded me of the atmosphere of India.

And, what a peculiar mode of behavior! I reflected.

There had been no communication on levels I could understand. Instead, they had shared a sort of intuitive knowing with those around them. It had been almost as if they were experiencing a comparable sensation, a similar altered state of consciousness.

Worst of all, they had rejected me. I had felt as though I were an intruder. They hadn't even tried to make me feel comfortable. *Well, I sighed with relief, at least I've got that out of my system. I know what I don't want to become. I don't want to block out the reality of the world, life, and people.* Thus I had rationalized away the disappointment of that earlier London experience. For, although my conclusions had been basically sound, they had risen out of the need to soothe my feelings of failure rather than to honestly look at the situation, and therefore did not stop me from trying drugs again in a different environment.

So, there I was a few months later in the Bahamas, lethargically stretched out on the white sands, oblivious to the existence of the surrounding world, worshiping the sensations and experiences that accompanied my constant use of drugs.

My capacity for critical evaluation was gradually slipping away. Instead, I was beginning to believe in my own world of make-believe. Not only was I losing the art of analysis, but principles I once held dear were beginning to blur in my mind. Time and space were becoming fuzzy. Days merged into weeks and months. The inclination to make responsible decisions and pursue the possession of such things as a steady income, security, a job, and a place to live no longer seemed to be important. I began drifting and didn't realize I was adrift.

The Island Development Project came to an end, and our collective services were no longer needed. My fantasies of retiring on this little piece of secluded paradise came to an abrupt end, too. But my guardian angels (as I had been taught to believe in Roman Catholicism) were protecting me. Or was it the good "karma" I was beginning to learn about through my philosophical hippie friends?

America

With fatalistic abandon, I submitted to the "friendly" circumstances of my continuing saga. I flew into Miami, Florida. There I was welcomed by new acquaintances, and it didn't take me long to get settled. I was about to begin yet another new life—this time in America.

I bought a little VW car. I named it "George" after my father, and George Harrison, my favorite member of the Beatles. My constant companions "George," "a little bit of dope," and myself drove around the areas surrounding Miami. We found our way from Florida's east coast and its spectacular Fort Lauderdale, through the fascinating Everglades and the fabulous keys to Key West.

Again, I saturated myself in nature's beauty. By now, I was believing myself to be one with the sunsets, the ocean views, and the lush tropical vegetation. I imagined myself blending with the beautiful colors and aromas of exotic flowers, the abundance of blossoming trees, and the enormous ancient Banyans—East Indian fig trees that characteristically drop their cobwebby branches to the ground to root. They reminded me of the India I had loved as a child. All this beauty seemed to confirm the *oneness* of the universe to me.

My artistic temperament led me to buy sketchbooks and crayons and spend many hours in the botanical gardens attempting to capture the sheer elegance of all I saw. Never before had I felt so free, so in tune with nature, or so "at one" with its beauty. I believed that all my senses were more alive than they had ever been before. I seemed to be developing another dimension of astuteness, allowing me to experience "everything-being-part-of-everything," a universal oneness.

After living in many homes with different families, I eventually rented a cozy little apartment in a bohemian location called Coconut Grove. Soon, visiting English photographers, working on various advertising and promotional projects, hired me for some modeling jobs.

I looked for freelance art work whenever I needed additional money. I was also employed, due to my English accent, as a hostess to an exclusive private club. There I met a variety of interesting people who helped to expand my social awareness of America and its foreign (to me, anyhow) customs.

Intriguing American football games made me an ardent supporter of the Miami Dolphins. Drive-in movies got me hooked on hot buttered popcorn. And I became a hysterical rock concert fanatic. The messages and deafening amplification of rock bands got me addicted to music that aided in altering my consciousness. Back in the days before CDs, or even cassette recordings, I would spend hours consumed with listening to rhythmic vinyl record albums, unaware that they infiltrated my subconscious with mystical religiosity. For instance, one of my favorites then—The Moody Blues album, *In Search of the Lost Chord*—had a colorful cover depicting reincarnation and elevation to god-consciousness through meditation. The songs reflect the use of drugs and meditation and belief in Hinduism, UFOs, and astral projection. With the sound of sitars and hypnotic music, I was led to knowledge of the power of the mantra (the repetitive chanting of the names of Hindu deities, vibrations, and other mysterious code words). Such albums tantalized my musical cravings. Many of the songs I loved confirmed the rightness of my drug experiences and my new sense of universal consciousness.

An insatiable desire for the thrills drugs gave had me rolling my first joint before I even got out of bed in the morning. Light-headed and lost in overwhelming sensations, I often found myself imagining that I was able to reduce my size to a pinhead or enlarge it so I could envelop the whole universe. I could merge with the universe, become part of it, and lose my identity completely.

I found myself being taken by faceless forces through different dimensions of consciousness, traveling through time and space. I felt very heavy at times, as if I would burst with the weight of my every blood vessel. In other instances I felt as light as the cotton-ball puffs of England's late summer dandelions, and could blow myself into oblivion.

Hinduism Disguised

I don't remember when I started the practice of Yoga or why. Perhaps it began to interest me during my grocery expeditions to the health food store. Dozens of notices on the door advertised an assortment of Yoga classes. Their claims attracted my attention: "More vigor, less stress, more calm, more strength, higher IQ, sexual prowess, and control over any weakness." Such claims alone may have convinced me to try Yoga.

Perhaps I was first intrigued by one of the little booklets I picked up at the supermarket checkout counter. Those publications convincingly assured me that Yoga was the most beneficial sort of home exercise and had no spiritual obligations. Or it might have been Richard Hittleman's early morning *Yoga for Health* television program, which combined exercise instruction with subtle philosophy that initially attracted my attention.

In any case, every morning I found myself sitting cross-legged in my living room with eyes closed, arms relaxed, and palms in my lap facing upward. Later I was to learn that touching my third finger to my thumb added greater energy to this mystical position. I would slowly begin my rhythmic breathing: controlled, shallow, and circular, concentrating on my breath going in through my nose and out through my mouth, down one side of me and up the other. This hypnotic performance powerfully took me beyond what I perceived as my limits. My imagination focused on an illusory object somewhere comfortably before me. Later I centered upon my *third eye*, believed by occultists to be lodged in the middle of the forehead and to be the center of psychic power.

Yoga, a practice that is at the heart of Hindu philosophy and religion, means to yoke. Its goal is to unite man with Brahman,

the Hindu concept of "God" (or god-consciousness). Brahman represents everything. It is seen as the all, the absolute. Brahman is both all good and all bad and is the power and the force of the universe—the god of India.

As my curiosity developed over the weeks and months, so did my Yoga exercises. Although they had started out as a physical practice, they were now subtly embracing Hindu philosophy and a mystical and spiritual dimension too. By the same method I had used to visualize my third eye into a reality, I also conjured up energy centers, known as *chakras*, which I perceived to be placed along my spinal column. Through mental gymnastics, I believed I was raising my psychic energy (said to be dormant) nestled in the lower extremities of the groin. Through imagination, I pushed the energies upward through my chakras, which I felt gave me maximum powers. Ultimately I trained these *energies* to fuse above, where I imagined my *third eye* to be, and created the most "peaceful" and "blissful" experiences.

I got thoroughly taken up in these mystical experiences, which consisted of a mingling of sweet music, blinding light, and colorful emanations. I sensed these were the results of a deep spiritual union between me and a cosmic consciousness or divine essence. I attempted to explain these experiences to others. My friends knew immediately what I meant. They likened it to the "ultimate cosmic sexual experience."

When I discovered sexual parallels to cosmic experiences, I found the two difficult to separate. Somehow, mystically, they blended together in my imagination and soul to satisfy (albeit temporarily, as I was to find out later) my deep longing to be accepted, needed, and loved. Whatever was happening, I was convinced that these manifestations were filling my emotional vacuums. They also anesthetized unwanted hurts.

My hunger for new emotional experiences led me more deeply into the introspection of Yoga and meditation. To my surprise, I began to realize I was experiencing the same thrills in Yoga as I attained on my drug-induced travels into altered states of awareness.

As my needs drew me into deeper dependency on these habits, I found I could no longer be sure of encountering pleasurable marvels. Instead, with more frequency, I had erratic hallucinations. Self-communion through deeper reflections gave me confused depressions. Contemplation of *self* further engrossed me in muddled complexity.

The more I attempted to escape through self-consultation, self-help therapies, psychology, psychiatry, and self-analysis, the more frustrated I became. My inner turmoil appeared to be insurmountable, but I had achieved a kind of outward control I didn't want to lose.

By my mystical revelations, I felt I had tapped into a hidden, secret knowledge within me. I believed I had acquired intuitive and psychic abilities, telepathy, and extrasensory perception (ESP). All these involved a mind-over-matter-and-senses power, which I began to fanatically cultivate.

I had already become quite proficient in astrology, the occultic study of the supposed influence of the stars on human affairs. Astrology gave me the ability to quickly summarize a person's character and predicament at any given time. I believed it enlightened me regarding my own personality and surrounding circumstances. At best, this analysis made me believe I had superior knowledge and gave me quite a sense of authority.

However, I also found these superstitions dictating how I should run my life and all its diverse encounters. My view of astrology controlled my emotional response toward certain people. I believed that some individuals would make less suitable friends than others because they fell into supposedly incompatible categories with mine.

Through my Yoga practice, I felt I had mastered psychokinesis and its counterpart, ESP. Both are forms of psychic control over circumstances and people. I remember some remarkable coincidences that took place after I had visualized them in my Yogic hallucinations. For example, if I wanted a particular job or desired that a certain thing take place, if I needed immediate money or wished to befriend a man to whom I had recently been introduced, I would simply project my needs into visions. More often than not, my visualization became a reality. I had erroneously become convinced that I had the power to alter my reality, when in fact it was demonic spirits that were at work in my life.

Once I remember scheming interior designs to make my little apartment more efficient for entertaining. I wanted a wet-bar to double up as a room divider and had a specific design in mind. I also wanted a little built-in corner desk for my art supplies. I needed to have some shelves custom-made to encase special knickknacks, as well as other odd carpentry jobs done. I was no handyman, but I recalled one of my friends was.

I visualized him approaching me and asking to do all the things I needed to have done. I pictured him working hard following my designs. I heard him volunteer his time and energy in exchange for love and friendship. In my mind I agreed with the deal, seeing nothing immoral or promiscuous in our transaction. I thought that my way of payment was fair exchange for his manual work.

That same afternoon there was a knock at my door, and there stood the friend I had been visualizing in my morning meditation! He said that he had felt me thinking about him and wondered if I needed anything. A couple of weeks later, all I'd wanted in the house had been built. And at that point, no longer needing him, I began to emotionally discard and ill-treat this friend. His tears and pleadings did not persuade me to continue the relationship. I didn't care that his heart was breaking. He had to go.

One with the Cosmos

I became frustrated and dissatisfied with my power to overlord and control people—especially in areas of romance. My infatuations were short-lived. They were fun while they lasted, but after I had wrung out all I wanted from the relationship, I would feel pressured by the emotional demands that a liaison calls for. While I had certain manipulative powers over others, I was very troubled that I could not always control my own desires and weaknesses. My frustration always drove me to end the relationship, even though I hated the emotional hassles. I created irrational and unreasonable melodramas, and I knew it. I also realized that instability had been rearing its ugly head for years in all sorts of situations, but I didn't know how to deal with it.

All I knew was that relationship after relationship failed to meet my desire for a deep and satisfying love. I pursued my illusive, intangible dream, not knowing how to catch what I was grasping for. Why was it that I could skillfully acquire jobs, money, travel opportunities, relationships, and even mystical, spiritual satisfaction, and yet could not quench the craving for love that kept me crazily searching?

Among the powers that were bombarding me, pulling me farther and faster into psychic realms, were out-of-body sensations. I found I could levitate and astral project (visit different places). I vividly recall once hovering in the sitting room of my parents' home in England. I was meditating in my room in Florida when I started floating away, unaware of where I was going. The next thing I knew I was eavesdropping on my parents' conversation!

Mum and Dad were talking about me. My father seemed lovingly concerned for my well-being, but the air was filled with tension. They were almost arguing. My father was reading a letter I had sent them. They were discussing my vulgar language, shocked by my angry confusion with life and hurt by my accusations regarding them.

At last I drifted away from the scene. I was disappointed and interpreted my parents' reaction with disdain, believing them to be bigoted and narrow-minded. Many months later I was to learn from my sister that my parents were most concerned about me. They were indeed hurt by my insensitive letters and shocking language.

Sometimes a whole day went by before I realized I had spent it meditating in my own "stoned" fantasy world. Or had it been the real world? I could no longer discern. But by now I didn't care. Whatever this netherworld was that had become a part of my reality, I didn't want to lose it. Unconsciously I was absorbing the basis of Hindu thought, that reality is *maya*, an illusion, and that illusion or imagination can be conjured into reality.

My seasons in Florida fused together. Lazy, sunshiny days of deep, royal blue skies merged into days of deluging rain and destructive winds out of gray skies. These rainy seasons, accompanied by intolerable humidity even on days that it didn't rain, brought back memories of India's heavy monsoons. In India, however, hundreds of people died in raging floods caused by the monsoons, and life was held so cheap that most showed no concern. That lack of concern had deeply moved me as a child, but as a young adult in the early 1970s, I had changed.

"Life is only life, and death is only death; both are temporary and inconsequential," I heard myself rationalizing to a group of likewise stoned friends. "We are here in these bodies for a brief moment in time, then our bodies die and change and we come back to this world in a new form, perhaps better, perhaps worse."

Cold, apathetic revelations like this were partly brought about through the use of drugs and partly through hours of upside-down reasoning with my new, avant-garde friends. Such concepts drew me to empathize with the mystical teachings on reincarnation, transmigration of souls, and other myths from India.

I found myself philosophizing much during these months. I compared, evaluated, and dissected new notions based on humanism and a sort of Westernized Hinduism. My friends and I lavishly spent time on being stoned, and, in that altered state of consciousness, we attempted to reason on topics in which we felt we had a grasp. We talked about religion, politics, environmentalism, healthy eating, fitness, and holism, just to mention a few.

Eat No Meat

My experiences of being one-with-the-cosmos confirmed *holism* for me. Not only were my body, mind, soul, and breath one identity, they were also part of the universe as a whole. I was one with not only my fellowman, but also with all animals and nature. "Because," I reasoned, "everything has energy, and that is a life form, all of it is of one substance. Therefore, I'm a part of everything and everything is part of me."

This thinking was reflected in my eating. Originally, my habits changed not for mystical reasons but because I desired to be healthy. I believed that the ultimate form of healthy eating was vegetarianism. So I converted from a hearty meat-and-fish diet to a vegetarian one. At first, I considered it a difficult fad that I would probably drop like most of my other ventures, but soon I got hooked on its philosophy.

"Purity in eating leads to purity in being, in essence, in mind, and in emotions" became my motto. This holistic guideline convinced me that my spiritual being and physical being were one. I deduced that through vegetarian eating, not only was my body being cleansed, but my soul too. I considered my stoic vegetarian efforts to be an extremely righteous gesture warranting awesome admiration from my bohemian friends. Today I know that the primary motivation behind almost all my accomplishments was to gain the approval of my peers.

The theory behind vegetarian eating as the highest form of purity led me to campaign tirelessly for animal rights. Many times I considered animal rights to be more important than human priorities. I didn't realize until years later that I was developing an attitude toward animals I had rejected while growing up in India. Some animals were becoming sacred in my eyes. And I was placing their value well above that of human beings.

The same attitude sparked my extreme attempts to protect the environment. Nature was a goddess, part of Mother Earth, to be reverenced and honored. Nature had to be allowed to survive, even at the expense of human needs. In my holistic reasoning, I saw the created as the Creator—I deified nature and man—but within that thinking I came to illogical conclusions. Some animals, humans, and parts of nature had higher priorities than others. At that point, I hadn't rationally thought beyond the fatalistic view that their *karma* had caused their predicament.

As a child, I had believed that creation had come into being through the sudden and divine intervention of God. By now I had shifted to the idea of evolution, the gradual process of development. It seemed to make more sense that life, animals, and man had slowly evolved. The soul and essence of everything was continual, and their actions and vibrations determined their present status and their future development. Naturally, I included myself in this cycle of "wholeness" or oneness, but I believed I was at the top of the evolutionary process.

I traveled many, many months on my spiritual journey, absorbed by my pilgrimage. My vision was to fulfill my own potential and power and thus to create a better me and environment. In doing this I would be able to influence my destiny and control my circumstances.

These might seem to be worthy causes. Without fully realizing it, however, I was actually placing myself in a godlike position of authority. My new idea of God was that of an encompassing, transcendent *Consciousness*. I perceived God as a neutral *allness*, much like a permeating energy of peacefulness and goodness.

In actual fact, I often got muddled in my new spiritual outlook, vacillating between a personal and an abstract god. However, I was a persistent student, genuinely seeking answers. One large, puzzling contradiction with which I was faced was this: I acknowledged that the *permeating energy* was predominantly good and that I was part of it, but I also recognized I had a lot of bad in me. How could my badness be a part of this divine goodness?

One day I brought this question before a visiting spiritual sage from India. He quickly gave me a satisfactory answer, which I happily absorbed into my philosophy. "It's not a question of whether you are good or bad, or whether 'God' is good or bad. It's more like good and bad are relative. They are two sides of one coin, part of the same whole, attributes that you and 'God' possess."

"Ah, now it is all clear to me."

So it was that I justified my morals and ethics. Everything became relative.

Hare, Hare Krishna

It was around this time of my life that I was to become extremely attracted to the vivacious activities of the Hare Krishna movement. Every Sunday a young group of charismatic Western-Hindu fanatics would gather at the Coconut Grove community park near my home. There they offered the most delicious and colorful spread of vegetarian food imaginable. The sights, smells, and tastes brought back memories of India's mouth-watering foods. I was lured back again and again.

Loudly amplified music filled the park and the streets around it. My fanatical interest in the world of music and sound enhanced the powerful seduction of the Krishnas' hypnotic rhythmic chanting. Somehow, partaking of their food, music, and energy made me feel obliged to absorb their philosophy too.

I spent hours reading their literature and discussing their beliefs. I learned of the power behind their chant of "Hare Krishna, Hare Rama." This mantra or prayer syllable has to be repeated at least sixteen times a day. This actually comes out to sixteen times

Hare Krishna followers chant *Hare Kresna, Hare Rama* in a busy street in Prague, Czech Republic in June 2006

108 rounds, because it has to be said as the devotee touches each of his 108 beads—beads that represent to him all the sounds of the creative force of the universe.

The disciple believes that his continual chanting and vibrating bring him into mystical contact with his deity.

The Krishnas' shaven heads, minus one long strand in the center-back of the crown, serve a far more practical purpose: with it, the gods can pull their disciple up to heaven!

I became intoxicated with the Krishna disciples' devoted discipline. I knew I lacked structure in my own life, and I craved it. The conviction and purpose, which I had lost along the way and now saw in the Krishnas, attracted me. Their dedication, zeal, and sense of achievement made me see the emptiness of my own nomadic wanderings. I wanted a goal again. I longed to believe wholeheartedly in something and to follow it uncompromisingly. I was vulnerable, willing, and ready to be a Hare Krishna devotee.

Although I had become disillusioned with certain aspects of Roman Catholicism, yet I was finding similarities between *that* religious system and my newfound philosophies. I sought to clear up my own confusions by developing an ecumenical reasoning, accommodating both Christian and Hindu schools of thought. This led to a sense of spiritual superiority for being "tolerant" both of Eastern and Western religions. I welcomed the idea that all paths led to the same God and that all beliefs were equal.

My enthusiastic and dedicated Hare Krishna instructors had come from Roman Catholic backgrounds much like my own. This made for an even closer spiritual camaraderie among us. Their persuasive encouragement to join their organization was very manipulative. Only my selfish desire to cling to independence and materialism prevented me from succumbing. My motives, however, also made me feel very guilty, thus creating a difficult dilemma for me.

Then one day, extraordinary circumstances brought the Hare Krishna hierarchy to the large, comfortable house in Florida that I shared with several friends. Dave, one of our number, was a handsome health fanatic with a lively sense of humor. He was on the professional tennis circuit, and his best friend was Canada's number-one-seeded tennis player. Dave had invited this Canadian celebrity to stay with us. At the same time, he had arranged a get-together with officials from the local Hare Krishna temple.

I was elated, anticipating the privilege of meeting such honored guests in person. I rushed home from work that day tingling with excitement. I felt that perhaps a deep spiritual revelation was about to change my life. Could all my questions be answered? Would I have the courage to commit myself to this unparalleled group of dedicated Western Hindus?

I haphazardly parked the car outside our house. Running through the front door, I leaped two steps at a time up the staircase to the large reception room. It had been specially dimmed. I was a little late and everyone was already gathered, sitting cross-legged on the floor. I rushed in breathless, but to my disappointment, I went almost unnoticed. I felt momentarily deflated by the cold response.

As my eyes got used to the darkness, I was able to examine the devotees with their shaved heads and saffron robes. Indian musical instruments were placed in front of them, and they looked intense and serious. Whoever spoke became extremely animated in his conversation. *That's why they ignored me*, I consoled myself, *they are absorbed in their spiritual instruction.* I calmed my emotions and gave them my undivided attention.

To my surprise, I noticed that Dave was sitting among the Hare Krishna devotees, garbed in saffron too. As the afternoon progressed, it began to dawn on me that he had been a disciple of these people for months. We, his fellow housemates, hadn't even suspected it. By sharing a house with him I'd learned he was a vegetarian and health nut, and did hours of meditation. But a Hare Krishna devotee? I was amazed! *Why had he hidden the fact from us? Why did he continue to play tennis and to be so materialistic?* To me, materialistic meant he was living well, earning a good financial income in professional tennis, and dressing like us "normal" people.

Later, when I questioned him, he admitted that he had wanted to give up everything and be totally dedicated to the organization. But he revealed that his superiors had advised him to continue in his profession. They had convinced him that tennis-playing was his unique calling from 'God.' So in obedience he had continued to compete in sports and had contributed his plentiful earnings to the group.

"This," Dave told me, "is the most helpful way of serving God and providing for the development of God's movement." When he noticed my cynical expression he concluded, "Well, it's exactly what George Harrison is doing in his service to Krishna."

"Yes, I suppose so," I said with resignation.

George Harrison had recently denounced TM (Transcendental Meditation). Many suspected that he had publicly denounced Maharishi Mahesh Yogi, its founding guru, as the fool in the Beatles' song, "Fool on the Hill." The famous Beatle now felt that His Divine Grace Bhaktivedanta Swami Prabhupada, founder of the Krishna movement, was the true guru. Consequently, he was vigorously promoting his new experience through his musical talents.

I became too confused to argue the morality of it all with Dave. After all, George Harrison was my hero. His testimony and songs on mystical Hindu revelations had influenced me tremendously, along with millions of my peers. Empathizing with George's love for India, I had begun accepting his alluring views of Indian consciousness. I had felt comfort in knowing we experienced the same drug sensations. I had even followed his fashion trend, adopting a sort of Western-Indian look.

George is different, I argued with myself. *He overtly admits to being a Hare Krishna devotee. But here is clean-cut, straight Dave, secretly donating all his income to this group. Why doesn't he admit his spiritual affiliation?* I was disappointed that these austere, priest-like devotees weren't in the least bit interested in money. The Krishnas had preached quite the opposite to me. It was their very argument against materialism that had persuaded a materialist like me to want to change. It had been that very challenge I had found so appealing.

But, I recalled, *it was the Krishna hirelings who had talked to me so sincerely in the park. They're just naive followers trying to win souls. Now I'm face to face with their elite government, and they seem more worldly.*

I began looking at them more critically.

I soon found that those Hare Krishna officials were gathered in our dimly lit room with only one purpose in mind—to convert the tennis celebrity from Canada. They gave him undivided attention, wholehearted conversation, and warm smiles. They had an answer for every one of his questions. They even let his mocking and ridiculing comments pass seemingly unnoticed. I felt embarrassed at times by the cold sarcasm that oozed from him. It was obvious that the temple leaders were intent on capturing this star regardless of his flippant banter.

Meanwhile there was I—a genuine seeker, longing for answers. My sincere inquiries were dismissed with the same disregard shown to the Canadian's rudeness. I was blatantly ignored.

Slowly the whole picture began to emerge. At first, I couldn't believe my own reaction. *I must be jealous and bitter because they are neglecting me and paying attention to him.*

But the longer the afternoon went on, the more I could see why the temple leaders were there. They wanted our Canadian houseguest's money!

What about me? My eyes stung with tears. *I truly want to be part of you. He doesn't. I'm prepared to join immediately. I want to submit, to dedicate myself to the worship of Krishna, to wake at four o'clock each morning and pursue all the temple rituals. I will beg on the streets. I will give up all I have and become stripped and poor and humble for you.* Heartbroken, I realized my all wasn't enough for them. I felt rejected and bitterly hurt.

Eventually, the temple officers recognized their impasse with "Mr. Canada," and they appropriately changed the mood. Suddenly they started singing. Ecstatically they clapped their hands and wagged their heads, accompanied by the jingling of cymbals and rumbling of drums. The whining Indian sitar started up. Its melancholy tone added to my pain. Tears rolled down my cheeks. My elusive spiritual butterfly had flown by, having no desire to settle on my love-starved, longing soul.

Seven

Love in America

Our camera crew drove us deep into the heart of the Florida Everglades. The sun was blistering, the humidity making the air heavy. I was engrossed in the hubbub and excitement of a TV commercial shoot. Our product was a European martini. It was a chic, fun assignment.

Just before we wrapped it up for the day, a handsome, blue-eyed male model flashed a sparkling smile in my direction. I crumbled. My legs along with my heart turned to jelly. From that moment on, Denny wooed me relentlessly.

As the weeks progressed into months I found myself more and more enraptured with this dashing Casanova. I was joyously flattered by his amorous advances. He was without doubt an all-American catch—quite unlike anyone I had ever encountered before.

Denny had made a name for himself playing college foot-ball, and wherever we went we encountered his ex-girlfriends. He acknowledged their presence with all the charm befitting a gentleman, but he always let everyone know he was with me. This put me on cloud nine.

Denny was a boat broker and represented owners of expensive yachts moored in Florida's many waterways and channels. We would often go together to meet his clients. It gave us the opportunity to drive through country sunshine together, immersed in happiness.

In addition to his successful boat business, Denny was also an extremely popular fashion model, involved in many glamorous projects. He would try to include me in his travels whenever possible. Before long, I was his daily companion. Life was worth living again!

I wanted to reciprocate his love in every way I could. I tried to be the best person in the world for him. I longed to give him the best experiences, the dearest memories, and the most faithful dedication I could muster.

Falling Out of Step

Our fairy-tale romance absorbed me until I was struck with an unexpected calamity—my United States visa ran up against complications and I was given twenty-four hours' notice to return to England. Panic set in. Denny and I had spent every minute of the last few months together. The impending separation caused my life to crumble around me. No amount of pleading with the immigration authorities helped. Heartsick, I flew to London. Weeks later found me still in England, unable to accelerate bureaucratic paperwork and return to my sweetheart.

With passionate resolution, we decided to meet in Canada, where I did not need a visa. We would make a home for ourselves there. Reunited, we attempted our alternative Canadian lifestyle, but within a few weeks we had to concede it was a failure.

Denny had moved up from Florida to Chicago, where he could continue his fashion modeling and in time earn a reasonable living to maintain the two of us. He lived with his parents in Chicago's suburbs and commuted over the American-Canadian border between jobs to be with me. We both desperately tried to find work in Canada, but to no avail.

With these circumstances frustrating our intense desire to be together, we decided that our only option was to smuggle me across the American border. So one afternoon, with fearful hearts thumping, we drove into the United States illegally. We accomplished this mission safely, without incident, and with great relief. At last, we knew everything would be wonderful again, and we set out to regain the happiness we had known.

At first, sparse funds forced us to live with Denny's parents. This was a very obvious strain for them, and created horrible tensions between us all. His family felt understandably embarrassed by what they saw as immoral cohabitation under their own roof. They repeated the time-honored question, "What will the neighbors think?"

Their reactions and comments made me feel guilty, of course, but my guilt was not related to any supposed immorality. Denny and I certainly did not see our behavior as being immoral—after all, we were in love. No, my guilt stemmed from the resulting rift between us all, although I tried to blame it on the narrow-mindedness of his conservative-thinking family. But this state of affairs accelerated anxieties between Denny and myself.

A few weeks later, with reconciliation in mind, we moved out of the suburbs to a small apartment near Rush Street in Chicago. There we tried to pick up the threads of our relationship again. Unfortunately, the strains of the previous few months had taken their toll. I came to realize with great remorse that I was unqualified to live up to my high hopes for this partnership.

For the first time in my life, I was confronted with a hopeless disillusionment with myself, and neither drug trips nor occultic adventures could change the hard facts.

I was unable to work because I didn't have a legal work permit. My dependency on Denny for every penny made me feel inadequate and degradingly "kept." His growing reputation as a top model called him out on constant business, and that only made me feel more insecure.

I knew he was hobnobbing with the "beautiful people" in glamorous locations, and I was consumed with irrational jealousy and possessiveness. This became a catch-22 situation—I needed to be with the man I loved, but I was unable to cope with the tensions within our relationship.

I knew that my own inadequacies were forcing an estrangement between us, but instead of taking responsibility for them, I blamed everyone but myself.

Naturally, I didn't want Denny to look too closely at my shortcomings—I longed to appear perfect in his eyes, so I blamed my parents for not grounding me

in love. I angrily decided that they had provided me with no adequate family environment. My problems were the result of parental abandonment—the years at boarding schools, the constant chaperoning by nannies, aunts, and foster guardians. My list of grievances was endless—it exhausted even me.

Although our love affair was deteriorating rapidly, these depressing undercurrents were known only to Denny and myself. Judging by appearances, no one would have guessed our inner turmoil. On the surface, we appeared to be infatuated children, madly in love with each other. We seemed happily entwined in a unique relationship, and in a way, we were.

Through tears, I would sometimes look at the photographs of our days in Florida, Canada, and Chicago and be swept away all over again by our love. The fun and laughter we had shared was vividly captured in those albums. But reliving the good times made me all the more restless. Why couldn't I maintain equilibrium?

Prayer to an Unknown God

One bitterly cold morning, after yet another sad quarrel, my hopelessness drove me to roam the Chicago streets. I walked and walked, feeling lost, searching for a solution. As though drawn by a magnet, I found myself walking along a well-maintained path, lined with an abundance of blossoming shrubs. I loved flowers, and in my sadness they comforted me. I glanced up the pathway to see where it led and noticed a large wooden door. As I continued to follow the line of the building skyward, I realized I stood in the shadows of a beautiful, cathedral-like church.

The sanctuary silently beckoned me to enter. I was glad for the invitation to a secluded place. Cautiously I pushed open the heavy door. It was warm and inviting inside—the Roman Catholic surroundings were familiar. With ease I walked over to the *holy* water font in the cloister and dipped my forefingers into the sanctified water. I made the sign of the cross from my forehead to my lower chest, from my left shoulder to my right—an automatic gesture to cleanse myself before entering the church. I saw the sanctuary lamp hanging above the altar, glowing red, indicating that the *Blessed Sacrament* was reserved in the tabernacle, the boxlike container placed on the altar. The flame gently reminded me to maintain an attitude of reverence. As a child, I had been taught that the actual body of Christ was on the altar, concealed in the form of the bread. I genuflected deeply before the altar and walked up to kneel at the rails.

For a few minutes, I felt very religious. After so many years, the customs had come back to me quite naturally. Then suddenly, I was at a loss. I had completed all the introductory rituals. *Now what should I do?* I was too wounded to launch into the formal, ritualistic prayers. I was too weary to think through ceremonial words. "Oh God," I sighed deeply with a real sense of inadequacy. "Please help me to become a better person. I've tried so hard to improve and change and to give Denny love the best way I know how. But it's not good enough. I want to know how to love."

Having nothing more to say, I looked up. For the first time, I noticed an enormous wooden cross hanging down from the high, domelike ceiling. It seemed to be reaching down to me.

I don't know how many hours I knelt gazing at that cross and pondering its significance. My heart melted as I thought of the agony and mutilation that the Person on the cross had gone through. *I wish I had that kind of attitude*, I thought, *that kind of sacrificial love.*

Several days later, Denny took me on one of his modeling assignments. A Sears Department Store commercial was to be shot in a cheerful green park near Lake Michigan. During a break, some of us were sprawled on a blanket enjoying a picnic luncheon. Two of the models were deeply engaged in a dialogue about God. "Jesus Christ is the only way to God," I overheard Charles say to John.

"What an outrageously intolerant statement that is!" I snapped back at Charles before realizing I was rudely interrupting the conversation. "All paths lead to God," I argued. "How can you make God so small that He can only communicate through one path? What about all the African and Red-Indian tribes in the middle of the jungle that don't even know about the Jesus path?"

I felt an angry, indignant knot grow inside me as Charles tried to answer my questions from a biblical viewpoint. "And as for using the Bible as a point of reference and authority," I retorted, "what about all the other great scriptures and spiritual teachings. Are you dismissing their wisdom as not being the truth just because they contradict your Bible?"

The crew called everyone back to work, ending the debate. I felt arrogantly victorious. Charles had been unable to answer me satisfactorily. Little did I know that Charles' words had sunk deeply into John's heart and that he would soon move into a powerful spiritual relationship with the biblical God. Nor had I any idea that, from that afternoon on, Charles was daily lifting me up in prayer to his God. Weeks later I learned that he had been asking God to break my hard veneer and reveal Himself and His Son, Jesus Christ, to me.

A few days later John pleaded with us: "Please come with me to meet some new friends."

Denny and I had turned him down three times previously and were uncomfortable doing it again. We were also exhausted, and we both felt we were coming down with a flu bug.

"All right," we finally conceded, "but we can't stay long."

We jumped into the car and began our journey to Old Town, Chicago. With plenty of extra time, we decided on a detour to enjoy the night lights of the city. I've always loved sparkling lights, especially when reflected in water. They remind me of childhood evenings when my parents would drive us around Calcutta's waterfronts to watch "the big ships that come in from all over the world."

I was immediately captured by the sights of Chicago's vivacious nightlife. Proselytizing homosexual men touted for business with flippant badinage and feminine antics. Transvestites pranced about in outrageous garb while prostitutes strutted the sidewalks like beautiful peacocks, proudly displaying their sexual allure. Pornographic shops flashed bright neon signs advertising outrageous films and gimmicks for pleasure.

Billboards glamorized cigarettes, liquors, and beauty aids. Crowded restaurants and bars looked inviting. Busy sidewalks were filled with animated, trendy people. All the commotion made for a chaotic excitement which appealed to my senses.

We detoured along chic Michigan Avenue, where world-renowned designers offer expensive, prestigious fashions. My eyes feasted greedily on every beguiling piece of apparel in every department store window.

We then cruised along scenic Lakeshore Drive on our way to Old Town. The breathtaking view of Chicago's skyline from Lake Michigan is to me one of the most beautiful vistas in the world.

My adrenaline was pumping. I felt glad to be alive and reassured that I was in the center of the real world. Meanwhile, John was explaining how he had discovered the newly acquired friends we were about to meet.

They had approached him in the touristy streets of Old Town, a community reconstructed by creative hippies and artists in the midst of sordid ghettos. "It's just an informal get-together," John explained. "We'll be in the heart of the arts-and-crafts scene. They meet at the back of a bookstore."

We arrived at a brightly lit bookshop that radiated an air of friendliness. My insatiable artistic drive had me gravitating toward the fascinating graphics, cover designs, and illustrations of the displayed books. I wanted to continue browsing, but John said, "No, Caryl. We're really late now. Why don't you look on the way out?"

So we walked through the shop and arrived in a cozy back room. Everyone glanced up and smiled at us warmly. They welcomed John with special enthusiasm and moved around to make room for the three of us. *What a friendly bunch of people!* I smiled to myself. An overwhelming sense of love was everywhere. It was almost visibly tangible in the room.

As we settled on the floor, I noticed I was surrounded by glowing faces. *They must be high on some potent dope*, I thought, glancing around to see who had the joint. But I couldn't smell that familiar marijuana smell.

There was no movement now, and everyone's attention went back to the speaker, who had obviously been interrupted by our tardiness. To my amazement, no one had made us feel uncomfortable about our late entrance. *How considerate*, I reflected.

Like the others, my attention focused on Richard, the speaker. He was a skinny, rather anemic-looking hippie with straight, stringy hair hanging loosely over his shoulders. He wore faded blue jeans, much like everyone else in the room.

Richard spoke quietly, with a gentle Canadian accent; I couldn't get the gist of what he was saying. My eyes wandered to the others. They were all peaceful bohemian-looking types, quite different from any group of people I had ever been with before. I was attracted to them and wondered why. *Perhaps it's because they're so natural and unaffected*, I thought. *No airs and graces. And they're very friendly.* Everyone was alertly listening to Richard and his message. *What on earth is so engrossing?* I wondered.

As my eyes moved toward Richard again, I tried to grasp what he was talking about. Although he looked insignificant, he spoke with strong authority and conviction. He picked up a well-worn book sitting beside him and started reading from it. It was really interesting. I wondered what the book was.

He flipped through the pages as though he were dealing with

an old friend, darting from one section to another, comparing chapter with chapter. I was intrigued.

As the discussion developed, I was surprised to realize that the book was the Bible! I had never thought the Bible to be so interesting. Outside of the religious education of my school days, I had never been exposed to a group of contemporaries discussing the Bible. But here was Richard, illustrating through biblical history how God spoke to people; how He led their lives through circumstances; how He directed them to a place where He could commune with them; how He brought them into a personal relationship with Himself. *Hmm, I reflected, this fellow speaks as though he knows God as a personal Friend. God isn't a personal entity . . . is He?*

All this was quite perplexing. I had grown used to the notion that "God" was a mixed assortment of "essence," a massive and impersonal but friendly "energy" available through an existential experience. I also knew from my Roman Catholic upbringing that God was an awesome Father figure approachable through prayers, good deeds, and a host of dead saints who were with Him in Heaven. But what God was this?

Who Is This Jesus?

Before I knew it, an hour-and-a-half had passed. The meeting was coming to an end. Richard closed it with an invitation to everyone to pray. He, along with the others, bowed their heads, and there was a spontaneous time of informal conversation between those present and their *listening* God. I looked around the room to see if anyone else was as amazed as I was by this very unfamiliar behavior, but all were absorbed in deep communion, their eyes closed. They spoke to God respectfully and on a one-to-one basis. They were simply bringing their thanks, praise, love, and worship to Him.

My last discussion with a group of religious people had been with the Hare Krishnas over a year earlier. I still remembered the coldness of their hearts, and couldn't help contrasting it with the love I witnessed here. *What is the difference?* I kept asking myself.

Perhaps it was to get my question answered, or perhaps it was because I felt a touching sense of gratitude toward the humble speaker, but after the prayer time I found myself moving through the little group toward Richard. As he smiled at me questioningly, I fumbled for words to express my thanks, which he acknowledged modestly. Then he asked a strange question: "How long have you known Jesus Christ as your personal Savior?" I was totally stumped. I didn't really understand his question. *Savior? What do I need with a Savior? From what do I need to be saved?* I thought to myself. "Well, I have been a Roman Catholic all my life," I replied hesitantly.

He tried the same question again, but this time with a different slant: "When did you accept Jesus Christ as your Lord?"

"Er, well, I don't know," I replied, a little puzzled. I had never really considered Jesus as my Lord. I had certainly prayed to Him as "Lord," but I hadn't thought through what that meant.

Richard was very patient with me. He gently probed further, "Well, do you believe that Jesus Christ is the Son of God and that He died for your sins on the cross?"

I contemplated his question. Vividly, I recalled the giant wooden cross I had prayed under just a few weeks ago. I remembered gazing for hours on that tired, thin body so pitilessly nailed there. I remembered my prayer, begging God to teach me what love was all about.

"Do you know that God loves you so much that while you were unaware of Him, and while you were still a sinner, He came down from His heavenly pedestal and became a human, Jesus Christ? He came to save you, to forgive you, to cleanse you, and to bring you into a relationship with His Father."

My whole being clung to Richard's every word.

"His unconditional love for you is so strong that He took all the punishment for your sins without the guarantee that you would even accept Him. And yet your sins separate you today and for all eternity from being in the presence of God."

I frowned as a question formed in my mind. *I have been in the presence of God. What does he mean that my SINS separate me? I've experienced God!*

Richard noticed the furrows on my brow and smiled.

"God's character is made up of only goodness. He can't unite with anything bad. Jesus, because He's a member of the Godhead and sinless, is the only One able to cleanse you from your sins. You wouldn't use dirty water to wash soiled garments, would you? Only pure, clean water would purify them completely. So it is with God's method of salvation. God gave us Jesus, His only-begotten Son, to wash us clean, so that all those who believe in Him can be declared blameless. Because of Jesus, we're able to have a personal relationship with His Father."

I was shocked by the simplicity of God's loving plan. *A free gift of redemption? And all I have to do in exchange is believe that HE has done it ALL?*

I was dumbfounded. I remembered the hundreds of times I had completed the circuit of the Stations of the Cross around Roman Catholic churches worldwide. Hadn't that made me more righteous in God's eyes? What about all those Holy Days of Obligation when I attended Mass? Didn't that raise my rating in God's score book? What about those numerous hours I had prayed—with automatic emptiness—the hundreds of rounds of the Rosary? Hadn't those prayers helped reduce the amount of punishment I deserved? Had all my efforts been to no avail toward my eternal destiny? Why had the *Mother Church* made our religious obligations so impossible to fulfill? No wonder I had looked elsewhere for peace and hope!

I stared at my feet and shuffled them around slowly, well aware of a heavy silence. I felt grateful that Richard kept quiet so I could be alone with my thoughts.

At last I looked up. "Do you mean that what Jesus did on the cross is completely sufficient and that He is all I need?"

Richard nodded gently.

I shook my head. "I don't know," I sighed.

I found it difficult to believe it was so uncomplicated. And there was such a stubborn knot of pride in me.

Suddenly, almost miraculously, I could see the futility of all I had done for so many years. Here I was, this filthy rag, trying to cleanse myself through my own dirty-water methods!

Still my pride was fighting. "But, Richard, I had such wonderful experiences of being in the presence of 'God.' I saw him and touched him. I talked to him and he talked to me!"

Richard smiled knowingly. I was to learn weeks later that he had had the same encounters on drug trips and the same occultic experiences as I'd had. "It is all a counterfeit," he said. "There's a spiritual battle taking place in the airwaves of this world. The god of this world is the devil. He's known as Lucifer, which means "an angel of light" (II Corinthians 11:14). He's a liar and a deceiver. He offers us enticing experiences so we won't leave his world and turn to the real King of all creation, who gives us knowledge and understanding of true freedom and love.

"The Bible says, 'Be on the alert. Your adversary, the devil, prowls about like a roaring lion, seeking someone to devour.' It's Satan's job to give us whatever pleasures we want to experience, as long as they keep us away from the truth."

"But how do we know what the true God is and what the false god is if the experiences and feelings are so similar?" I asked.

"By reading the Bible. The Bible is the true Word of God." He picked up his Bible from beside him and thumbed through that faithful friend with affection. "And by dependence on the Holy Spirit." Richard read John 16: 12-14:

> I have yet many things to say unto you, but ye cannot bear them now. Howbeit when he, the Spirit of truth, is come, he will guide you into all truth: for he shall not speak of himself; but whatsoever he shall hear, that shall he speak: and he will shew you things to come. He shall glorify me: for he shall receive of mine, and shall shew it unto you.

"Well, never before has all this been explained to me in this way," I proclaimed with total wonderment.

"Me neither," said Denny. I was aware for the first time that he was at my side. I looked at him, bewildered.

"Isn't this all incredible? Have you been listening to it all?"

"Yes," Denny nodded.

Richard said to Denny, "Are you Roman Catholic too?" Denny nodded.

"Well, would you both like to ask Jesus right now to be your Savior and Lord?"

Oh, golly! I thought. When it came to the crunch to make a decision, I felt suddenly flustered and embarrassed. *Is this going to be some complicated ceremony?*

Richard picked up on our nervousness. "Just talk to Him simply. Admit that you are a sinner and that you want to be forgiven. Thank Him for dying in your place and for taking the punishment that you rightfully deserve. The Bible says if you confess with your mouth that Jesus is Lord, and believe in your heart that God raised Him from the dead, you will be saved (Romans 10:9). Don't just accept Him as your Savior. Ask Him to be your Lord too."

"You said that before, but I don't know what you mean by 'Lord.'" I felt somewhat agitated and didn't quite know why.

"Let Jesus make your life's decisions. Let God's plan control your life." He smiled and added, "You've had the chance to be the pilot of your life until today. You probably haven't done a very good job of steering, have you?"

My eyes lowered. Tears fell to the ground as I was overcome by a sense of shame.

"Well," Richard said lovingly, "allow God to take over. See what He has in store for you. Read the Bible. Ask the Holy Spirit to lead, direct, and guide you in all you do, say, and think. Kick your own ego off the throne of your life and allow God to sit in His rightful position."

Denny and I looked into each other's eyes, searching for approval. We knew we needed something powerful to mend our broken lives. We squeezed each other's hands tightly for comfort.

Together we bowed our heads. I remember weeping gently as I prayed to God saying, "Dear Jesus, I'm so sorry for having rejected You in the past, and for making such a mess of my life. Thank You so much for loving me, and for forgiving me. Thank You for giving Your life on the cross in order to set me free. I give my life to You. Please come into my heart and take control."

I felt a great sense of relief. What did we have to lose by giving our *old* lives over to God? As it turned out, everything.

Jesus answered, Verily, verily, I say unto thee,
Except a man be born of water and of the Spirit,
he cannot enter into the kingdom of God.
That which is born of the flesh is flesh;
and that which is born of the Spirit is spirit.
Marvel not that I said unto thee, Ye must be born again.
John 3: 5-7

Eight

A New Heart

Denny, Richard, and I walked out of the back room into the brightly lit bookshop. Many of the Christians who had been at the Bible study were milling around the book displays. I started to do the same. Suddenly, I could see that all the titles related to Christianity and to the Christian's walk with God. All around me were Bibles, Bible stories, and devotional books.

This whole bookshop is devoted to Christian books! I was astounded! *How on earth could I have missed noticing that when I first came in?* I whirled around on my heel, taking in a panoramic view of the shop. It was cluttered to overflowing with Christian paraphernalia. *It's obviously a religious bookshop! How could I have been so blind?*

This was my very first revelation as a new Christian. In what a humorous way God had worked to get me to a place where I would hear what He wanted to say. He knew how antagonistic I was toward the Bible and toward Jesus Christ, His Son. He had blinded me to my Christian whereabouts so I would go into the meeting with an open mind and heart.

Only *I* would ever fully appreciate the significance of this. Only *I* knew how passionate I was about books—their cover designs and titles, their illustrations and graphics. Only *I* realized how readily artistic detail was computed into my memory bank for future professional use.

"You are a miracle-worker," I muttered to God under my breath, somewhat amused by the incident. "I understand a little bit about Your power already. You got the blind to see and You got me to lose my sight."

I could also see that God had allowed us to be delayed for the Bible study. That way we missed all the introductory prayer and Bible explanation. He knew those preliminaries would have quickly sent me walking out the door.

Waiting for Denny and Richard to join me, I had time to gather my thoughts. As I began to comprehend how carefully God had worked, my heart overflowed with a sense of warm gratitude. *How kind You are. How gentle. How thoughtful in every detail.* I was filled with the most incredible assurance of God's love toward me and His acceptance of me. *Imagine wanting a relationship with me after all these years that I've been so rude and antagonistic toward You!* I marveled at His friendship and how it compared to relationships with people who had rejected me in the past.

Now I have an example of love to base my future relationships on . . . I stopped in my tracks at the way I was beginning to think. He was already performing a miracle inside me! *My thinking is changing. I am beginning to soften.*

Seeing . . . For the First Time

I felt as though a great big, spiritual vacuum cleaner had sucked out all my sins and removed a barrier of hardness from me. *God is beginning to melt me into a new being.* I was exhilarated at the prospect. This was His first answer to my prayer—the prayer I had prayed beneath the cross in the Catholic church. And that had been weeks before I had come to know Him as my personal Savior and Lord.

"Are you ready to go?" Denny came up behind me, laden with books. On top of the pile were two Bibles. Denny handed me one. "It's for you, with all my love."

"Start by reading the book of Romans," said Richard. "I'm sure you'll find that it answers a lot of questions for you."

We were surrounded by loving faces. These newfound friends were rejoicing with God at our new birth. They were all members of a Christian community in Chicago. They were to be a source of great strength as they surrounded us with their continuous prayers and encouragement during the next few weeks.

As we drove home, John, Denny, and I enthusiastically talked about all the surprises we had encountered that evening. I was bubbling over with happiness, looking out the car windows with new eyes.

All at once, our drive home began to take on a different significance. Scenes that had filled me with a sense of belonging only a few hours before seemed to estrange me now. Suddenly I felt a deep sadness. What was happening?

Then, I had responded favorably to the worldly attractions of the city. Now, I saw only emptiness in all the glamour. In retrospect, I realize God was giving me spiritual understanding: I had many weird hallucinations while involved in drugs and the occult, but this experience was a special insight from the Lord.

My heart was flooded with deep compassion for the people on the sidewalk with whom I had previously empathized. Then unexpectedly, and in shocking animation, I saw these people turn into walking skeletons! Their movements appeared chaotic, directionless; they seemed to wander, like lost, dead people!

"What is happening?" I cried out. I grabbed Denny's hand in fear. With a pounding heart I said, "God has suddenly put a pair of spiritual 3-D spectacles on my nose! I can see through people's skins, into their hearts and their spiritual insides. I feel as though I'm looking at the horrors of sin as God sees them."

The pornographic stores that had amused me earlier repulsed me now. The prostitutes and homosexuals filled me with conflict.

I saw the abomination of their sin and yet felt a desperate love for them as lost people. Was this how God felt as He saw the world and all its detestable characteristics? How loathsome the results of sin are to Him!

At the same time, I could see how mighty God's love for the human race is. He *could* wipe everyone out, but instead, He continues to sustain us. He wants everybody to have a chance to come into a personal relationship with Him.

Over the next several weeks, God demonstrated His power by breaking many of my habits and addictions. I was more than willing to let go of them, so He filled me with the strength I needed for deliverance.

My first release was from nicotine. I had smoked up to fifty cigarettes on some days and had tried to cut down or go without at other times, but I was unable to find the willpower I needed to give up smoking. I had had such a love/hate relationship with it. Now I was free!

My desire to be satisfied by the highs of drugs was immediately eradicated too. So was my need for alcohol. The joy and peace I experienced through my new relationship with Christ far surpassed any high I had ever had.

My wardrobe was filled to capacity with the latest fashions and accessories. I wanted to share my lavish overabundance with the less fortunate. So I packed most of what I had, filling many big garbage bags. I took them to the Christian community and left them there for distribution.

The pursuit of modeling, art, and my other professional fortes seemed futile now. Instead I burned with a desire to do full-time missionary work that would bring other people to a relationship with the living God.

But the most traumatic change of all started the very evening that Denny and I returned from the Bible study. We waved good-night to John and turned to go into our apartment.

In a desire to be obedient, almost the minute we walked inside the door, we reached for our Bibles. With unabated enthusiasm we promised each other to read Scripture together every morning and every evening. That first night we didn't even know where to begin.

"Well, Richard said to start at Romans," I said encouragingly, "so let's begin there." I looked in the index for the location of Romans while Denny closed his Bible in anticipation of listening to me read aloud.

"Hmm, there it is, quite near the end." I allowed the Bible to fall open, flipping through several chapters as I tried to find the right page number. To add to my dilemma, it was most difficult to separate the delicate leaves of the new Bible.

We laughed at my clumsiness and Denny said, "Just read the chapter in front of you." I did. The words carried the very hardest message that either of us could have heard. We didn't like it at all. We looked at each other and tried to dismiss the seriousness of God's warning. I closed the Book, and he turned off the light. There was a long silence. We were both deeply convicted by the message. He reached for my hand and kissed it.

"Good-night," he said.

"Good-night," I replied.

The following morning Denny took his Bible and with more caution opened it to a different section from the one I had read the previous night. To our surprise, although in a different context, the words of another author brought the same sober message. We went about our daily business with heavy hearts.

That night, with extra-special caution, I opened my Book in an area I knew to be quite far from the other unpleasant passages. But for the third time, and almost unbelievably, the Scriptures read out the same message.

God heavily condemned sexual promiscuity and adultery in the Bible, and it said He hated divorce. Without a doubt our relationship with each other was wrong before God. And so was another matter we had been toying with for several months. According to Scripture, God would not condone my divorcing the husband I had left behind in England some years earlier, not even if my intention was marriage to Denny.

We battled with our consciences, our feelings, our emotions, and our young understanding of what it meant to be a Christian. We tried to re-stipulate and renegotiate the conditions of our newfound faith. But as we read the Bible more, we were more convicted.

A Difficult and Painful Decision

The seriousness of our decision to live for God was beginning to take effect. We wept at the hurt our inevitable separation would bring us. We had endured a separation only months earlier, and its agonies were still fresh wounds. After all we had gone through to get together again, did we have to separate forever?

Our hearts ached at the thought of my returning to a husband and relationship that I had hated. How could I give that marriage the same commitment that Denny and I would have shared?

Somehow, in spite of all the emotional pain, the Holy Spirit gave me incredible faith. I wanted to persist—to endure. He reminded me of the power that He had demonstrated in such a personal way on the evening of my conversion. Still, the cost of following Him was an extremely heavy burden for Denny and me. And soon choices would have to be made.

Over the next six weeks, Denny and I went to Bible studies with our new Christian brothers and sisters at every opportunity. We wanted to learn more and more from them and the Bible, and we craved fellowship and instruction. Sometimes we joined them as they worked among the hippie subculture, teaching others about the love of God through Jesus.

Denny and I were both struggling individually with the new life that God was placing before us. By now I was convinced I had to give up my illicit relationship with him.

I procrastinated my overseas marriage-reconciliation with Paul by coming up with seemingly important excuses, but all the while God was busy sweeping and cleaning out my old house. My conscience was nagging heavily and urgently about things I needed to do in order to be obedient to Him.

Besides my marital entanglement, there was my illegal residence in the United States. I needed to own up to the authorities. This brought the possibility of being sent to jail. Fortunately, that never happened.

At last, six weeks after our conversion, I left Denny and America. Despite the pain, God was enabling me to do what was right—to start a truly new life of living for Him rather than of seeking my own desires. How vastly different was that venture from all my others; instead of seeking pleasure, I was fearfully leaving behind everything I cherished. And yet, so great is God's power to work in us, that in the midst of great sorrow, part of my soul was singing. I had found the greatest treasure of all—knowing Christ! I knew I was about to face a hateful situation, but I already saw the power of God working in me, and I trusted that He would give me the strength to cope with it.

As it turned out, God graciously gave me more than the strength to cope. Though it had hurt Denny and I terribly to part, God had enabled us to die to our wishes and obey Him. As I continued to obey, I found that God, in His great mercy, gave me an unexpected new love for Paul, and a desire to make the marriage work.

Nevertheless, I struggled through my readjustment to England. It wasn't only my husband who was to reject me. My parents were extremely skeptical of my newfound faith as well. After my behavior over the past years, I could not blame them. I lived with my parents for several weeks while Paul was making his decision about our future.

During those days, I worked resolutely and hopefully to mend the broken relationship. I also tried to learn to follow God's leading, to hear His voice. I ventured into all the churches around our little village, searching for spiritual nourishment, but Sunday after Sunday, I heard only a worldly, non-biblical "gospel" being preached. There was never a mention of the living God, of His power and principles. *I must be the only Christian in England!* I thought, feeling very, very alone.

Day after day found me in my room crying, praying that God would show me what He wanted. I read the Bible constantly, learning the great historical accounts. Eventually, Paul made the decision that he did not want to live with me. I was puzzled and heartsick. He didn't want to make a marriage or divorce commitment at that time either. I had to wait on him and on God for that answer for three more years.

I was saddened that the marriage never did come to reconstruction. As time passed, Denny went his own way too. I was left alone with God.

In the meantime, I had begun to make work inquiries at charitable organizations. One day, through a set of astounding circumstances, I met a group of young dedicated American Christians. They were living in London, intent on spreading the saving message of Jesus. They begged me to join them.

So, at last, my course was set. The Pilot began to show me the charts. This time He would steer. I would simply trust Him. It would be His journey, not mine.

PART TWO

A NEW AGE/NEW SPIRITUALITY
East Comes West
1970s – 21st Century

Take heed therefore that the light
which is in thee be not darkness—
Luke 11:35

Nine

The View from Beulah Hill

The "House on Beulah Hill" was not an impressive residence from the outside. It bore no resemblance to the elegant accommodations I had enjoyed in my London jet-set years. But I moved in there with deep happiness.

My decision to live at the London outreach was part of my first missionary endeavor. It offered quite a different lifestyle from any I've ever experienced before or since. I dressed from a single suitcase of clothes and slept on my sleeping bag, which was laid on a mattress . . . sometimes! I had no job description—instead, I was available to do anything that needed to be done. I had no salary, but I had no bills either. I worked any and all hours on any and all days.

All this went totally against the "union rules" and basic human rights I had diligently campaigned for in the past.

I had once been a devout women's "liberator." I viewed male authority as being outrageously inhumane. Yet there I was, willing to help others, men or women, even by doing what I would have previously considered the most menial jobs. I also learned to accept the fact that others knew more than I and to submit myself to godly leaders who humbly submitted themselves to Christ's teaching and to each other. This was quite a change from the power-hungry or materialistic leaders I'd seen in the past. And I was learning all this without an attitude of condescension, reluctance, fear, or guilt, but with joy.

Every aspect of that *new* lifestyle was diametrically opposed to my old ways, yet I look back on those days with fondness. Despite the hardships, it was completely fulfilling. Despite our hectic hours of travel and work, I was never without food, clothes, or sleep. I was shown by others how Christians can live by faith in Christ. I began learning not to worry or to be anxious for anything. My hope and trust was in a Father-God who provided and cared for me with a deeply personal concern.

This was quite different from the faith I had held in my recent past. Then I had been at the mercy of an impersonal fate. I had been dealing with the cause and effects of my own *karma* or *vibes*. How wonderful to meet a personal God who was greater than anything in my past.

Depending on God to answer prayer according to His will was quite a departure from the faith I had had in my own power to accomplish my own will. Waiting on Him instead of going ahead with what I wanted brought new lessons in patience. Realizing that His solution was always far better than mine was humbling indeed.

And unlike me, God was considerate of other people's feelings. He made plans for me, but He made them with love for others and their needs in mind. This contrasted sharply to my own manipulative plans, which were made without consideration for anyone but myself.

This was a wonderful time: God's grace was poured out on my life in what I saw as miraculous ways, because they had nothing to do with my will or my wishes. One example of this was God's healing me from my past. It was an inner healing for me, but not in the sense this misused term usually conveys today. I had harbored grudges against my parents and other adults. I felt they had neglected me by sending me off to boarding schools from an early age. The lack of security that a normal family life provides was reflected in my inability to relate to people, especially in intimate relationships.

In the past, the quest for emotional health and self-improvement had led me to try endless therapies, psychological techniques, meditative counseling, Yoga, hypnosis, and other mind-over-matter and positive-thinking techniques.

From the hands of Jesus the Great Physician, however, is true healing, and the advice of Jesus the Wonderful Counselor surpasses any human technique or psychology. When I allowed Him to come into my life, He began the process of healing my inner hurts and insecurities.

There were no hours spent "psyching me up" to be more positive. There were no painful insights into the subconscious. No *rebirthing* techniques taking me back into the womb or prior lives. No *regression* leading me through altered states or reenactment of visualized events.

Jesus healed me through His power to forgive me and to help me forgive others. Jesus healed me by helping me to love those who had hurt me. These two gifts—forgiveness and love—were quite new to me. They did not come from *inner* or *outer* resources. Instead, they flowed from the character and power of the Great Healer Himself.

The by-product of my new ability to forgive and love was an inexplicable sense of peace. It was quite different from the mystical "peace" I had had before. The old tranquility that had passed for peace had been more of a detachment, a resignation, a sort of anesthesia. It had seemed like the real thing in its day, but now I could see how shallow it was. My reconciliation with the powerful, resurrected Christ had filled me with the biblical *peace that passes understanding*. And it all emanated from one beautiful realization—that Jesus loved me!

Darkness versus Light

Our Christian community was comprised of about eighty people. We came from all kinds of social backgrounds and represented over a dozen nationalities. Each person told a different and exciting story about how God's intervention had saved or rescued him from his or her previous lifestyle.

Over the months, bits and pieces were taken from each testimony and combined into a gripping stage play. We set our story to music and we acted it out in theaters throughout England, Europe, and America. Thousands of young people heard the Gospel message through the production.

The play's theme was spiritual foods and fads available in the marketplace of life. Our hero, through drama and song, tasted various earthly pleasures. He tried sex, drugs, Yoga, and vegetarian concoctions, concluding that no matter what he tried, he was always left hungry. Finally, he was given the *Bread of Life* in the biblical message of Jesus. The power of his conversion through faith in the unique God of the Bible was then portrayed.

In the final scenes, he met opposition and ridicule from his Haight-Ashbury friends. These characters raised the same questions that the audience members would be asking in their minds. Most of these were answered by the time the curtain came down. The rest were addressed by the cast, who made themselves available for interaction with the audience at the end of each performance.

All this was taking place in the early- to-mid-1970s. During those years the *Jesus movement* was growing and multiplying all over the world. Simultaneously, however, another movement was growing—that of spiritual counterfeits.

False god-men from the East, Indian gurus, were establishing themselves in the West with the teachings of "another spirit" and "another gospel," contrary to that of the Bible (II Corinthians 11:4). Just as millions were attracted to biblical truth, so millions were beguiled by error. Having come out of the combination of Eastern and humanistic philosophies and knowing its misleading errors firsthand, I was alarmed by the dangers of this escalating deception.

After each performance, whether in England, Europe, or America, I, along with other cast members, spent hours talking to the people in the audience.

The spectators came from diverse experiences. Many of them were rooted in an Eastern mysticism, which was blended with Western cultural thought and laced with Christian principles. During our conversations, I began to see how cunningly the two opposing views—Christianity and Eastern mysticism—were being merged, and how false religions resulting from that merging were integrated into our society.

I always looked forward to breaks in our show's itinerary because no matter where in the world we were, I was able to visit some of my friends from the past. By that time, many of them were well-ensconced in a life of drugs, Yoga, health trips, or "veggie eating" and had adopted various schools of Eastern thought.

Some had gone so far in their "conversions" that they dressed in the uniform of a group. I began to notice that more and more gurus demanded a dress code for their religious adherents. In the mid-1960s, the Hare Krishnas had been the only visible Eastern religious group. They were always recognizable by their shaven heads, orange robes (in India this color signifies renunciation of worldly lusts), and trance-like prance down various city streets.

In the mid-1970s and later, however, Indian "disciples" were blatantly worldly, despite the religious garb they wore. We would find them eating in fashionable restaurants. We would encounter them mingling at cocktail parties. They took part in theater and cinema entertainment. They shopped at chic shops and stayed in expensive hotels.

All this produced a strange dichotomy in my mind. Orthodox religious disciples in India automatically renounce materialism and life's pleasures. Their very commitment to a guru and his philosophical path accomplishes this. Whether in the East or the West, whether in the Brahmin priests of India or the Roman Catholic nuns of my Catholic school, I had been used to strict religious decorum.

I wondered how I would have reacted to the sight of those convent nuns making a noisy entrance to a cocktail party in their black robes of celibacy. I tried to imagine them brandishing drinks, dangling cigarettes, and flirting shamelessly. The Western contradictions of Hinduism I was seeing were just as outrageous, yet I was to encounter them increasingly.

One evening at a friend's "veggie" dinner party, I discovered another inconsistency of East-and-West fusion. There I met a couple of white Sikhs, members of 3HO (the Healthy, Happy, Holy Organization), a denomination of Hinduism that had gained much popularity in the West, especially in the United States.

The couple had been given new Indian names by their spiritual master, Yogi Bhajan, and had renounced their Christian names. Their guru, living in California and India, was a man of power, wealth, and influence—all of which is rejected among orthodox Indian gurus.

When I arrived back at Beulah House after this vegetarian extravaganza, I was famished.

"Give me meat!" I said, half-joking with the girls in the kitchen.

"Veggied out?" one of them giggled.

"You know, it's so good to be free from all that legalism," I sighed.

"Do you ever wonder if they're right?" The brown-eyed girl across the table looked serious. "I mean, maybe God would rather we didn't eat meat."

"No," I smiled at her. "In Genesis, God gave man dominion over the animals. In Exodus He fed His children with quails. In Leviticus He told the Jews which animals to eat. In—"

"Stop! You're not going through the whole Bible, are you?" We all laughed.

"Just two more points, and then I'm going to bed."

"I'm already convinced!"

"Well, just remember Jesus ate fish and lamb at Passover. And . . ." Here I stopped, flipped open my Bible, and read I Timothy 4, versus 1 and 3:

> Now the Spirit speaketh expressly, that in the latter times some shall depart from the faith, giving heed to seducing spirits, and doctrines of devils . . . Forbidding to marry, and commanding to abstain from meats, which God hath created to be received with thanksgiving of them which believe and know the truth.

While I am certainly not saying it is wrong to *not* eat meat, if the reasons for doing so are not spiritual or legalistic, there is nothing in Scripture that can back this up. The believer of the New Testament has been given the freedom to partake.

India Fever

In my Beulah Hill days, *India fever* was spreading through all social circles. At parties, I often overheard conversations among friends who had just returned from India. There they had learned from the *ancient wisdoms*.

One friend told me Sri Ramamurti had helped him "discover union with the Self by means of the inner music and the inner light." He had helped him "attain the experience of Nada Yoga, the vibration of life, light, and sound current."

Another young man said his guru had given him "the light of the inner guru." This *inner Self* was giving him visions and was his "inner guide for making decisions" and knowing what was "good and true."

Other friends reported with large, innocently glazed eyes the wonders of mystical India. They were somehow completely oblivious to India's horrible poverty, the result of an upside-down value system. They seemed blind to its unforgiving mind-set toward suffering and the less fortunate. That the Indian did not notice this was something I had learned to accept since childhood, but that Westerners should miss the unavoidable evidence of Hinduism's consequences was absurd!

Equally absurd was the bizarre trend that was taking some of my fashionable friends to the feet of a certain guru near Mumbai (Bombay): Bhagwan Shree Rajneesh (Osho), known as the sex guru. His followers wore varying shades of orange, from yellow to burgundy. These *sanyasins* raved about Rajneesh's profundities. His meditations and techniques "successfully combined Eastern mystical wisdom with Western psychotherapeutic teachings." The resulting experience, I was told, "far exceeds the highs of LSD or any other drug."

I listened sadly to these friends. They seemed to be losing all sense of reality. Instead, they believed that they were achieving a "higher actuality." My heart grieved for them because I had been on the same road to nowhere. I knew where its deceptive signposts led.

At a wedding reception, I was approached by a friendly man about my own age. He had a quizzical expression on his face. "Don't I know you?" he asked, seeming puzzled.

"I don't think so," I politely smiled. *I've heard that line a few times before*, I thought.

"No, I'm sure we've met." He was more insistent than I would have expected.

I looked him over carefully and shook my head. "Don't think so . . ."

"Well," he shrugged, "it must have been in another life."

"Oh," I laughed, "so you believe in reincarnation?"

"Doesn't everyone?"

"Well, not everyone. I don't. It's not such a terrific idea, you know. How can you be so sure you won't come back as a rat or a roach?"

He laughed hilariously. "Good question. No—that's the old-fashioned idea of reincarnation. No one thinks that way nowadays."

I envisioned the teeming multitudes in India who believe precisely that way and asked, "What do you believe?"

He seemed pleased with the opportunity to educate me. "You see," he began, "we're all on an upward path of evolution. And we're coming back as more highly evolved beings every time we're reincarnated. Eventually we'll be absorbed into the great cosmic wholeness."

"I don't think I'm following what you're saying."

"Each life," he patiently explained, "is part of the total life. Eventually, after we're spiritually refined, we'll become one with 'God'—the universal consciousness."

"That's interesting. But since I'm a Christian, I don't believe that way at all."

"Why not? Lots of Christians believe in reincarnation. Jesus was a reincarnation of the World Teacher, you know."

I felt saddened by his words. "You've got it all wrong. Jesus is the only-begotten Son of God. He died once and for all, our Christian Scripture teaches. Then He was resurrected, not reincarnated."

"It's the same thing, isn't it?"

"Not in the least. You see, the New Testament says, 'It is appointed unto man once to die, and after that the judgment.'"

"What do you mean 'judgment'?" The young man's curiosity was growing. "What's the judgment?"

"Well, the Hindu thinks he's procrastinating death's consequences by way of endless journeys through reincarnation. But in reality he's going to have to face God after he dies—to account for his rejection of Jesus. By contrast, the believer in Christ has confident assurance of a joyful eternal life spent in the presence of God."

"How do you know? How can you be sure?" He looked almost desperate for hope.

"I'm sure because Jesus Himself said it! He said, 'Whoever believes in Him should not perish, but have everlasting life.' Then He removed death's sting when He paid the penalty for our sins on the cross."

Thoughtfully, my new acquaintance paused. Then he said, almost to himself, "Eternal life . . . that's a completely different thing from reincarnation, isn't it? What do you think it will be like?"

"Well, the best part is the simple fact that we'll be in the presence of Jesus. He told His disciples, 'I go to prepare a place for you . . . where I am, there ye may be also'" (John 14:2-3).

He seemed lost in thought for a few moments. Then he smiled at me. "You know, I really did think I'd seen you before, but now that we've talked, I'm absolutely sure I've never seen you in this life—or any other one." He laughed.

I laughed with him. We said goodbye.

After my conversation with this appealing young man, my thoughts traveled to past years. Many times a casual dialogue with a man like that had led to dinner, to my place or his, to some sort of relationship, however short-lived.

Here was proof that my quest for love had ceased. Here had been a perfect opportunity to start a new romance, yet my heart had been elsewhere. *What a wonderful Lord!* I smiled to myself as I found my way home alone. Finding contentment was one of the greatest evidences to me of God's power and presence in my life.

In the Grasp of Deception

About this time, I received a sad letter from a friend in America. Another friend of mine had tragically died from an overdose of drugs. He had been an intimate friend. Saddened and shocked, I realized that "there but for the grace of God go I."

News came from another friend that her boyfriend had joined "the priesthood" of the Hare Krishna movement. They were to have been married. Now her life was crashing around her.

Meanwhile, I met a family whose offspring had left them to join a religious cult that claimed to be Christian. The leader told his followers that God was the greatest destroyer of the home and the family. I was deeply saddened by this heart-wrenching situation. It not only crushed the parents who were devout Christians, but it showed me that deceptions and counterfeits were no longer only the product of drugs or overtly Eastern or occult-based groups. Satan's lies were rapidly creeping into so-called Christian communities. The attacks of the devil were striking too close to home. I wanted to be involved in some kind of work to alert Christians to the dangerous teachings that were leading even God's "flock" away from the truth.

Along with a burning desire to inform and warn, I had an almost insatiable hunger for information. *How do the cults really compare with true Christianity?* I immersed myself in Bible study day and night. I also became absorbed in trying to understand the strange and distorted teachings of the cults, which was exhausting, heartbreaking work. But months of effort rewarded me with an ever-broadening perspective of counterfeit teachings and spiritual deception. I was amazed by my own diligence. *God is putting me through His own kind of schooling*, I remember thinking.

In less than a year's time, another miracle happened. The Lord of my life opened new doors and led me into exactly the kind of work that my heart desired. A generous businessman made the commitment to finance a cult-identifying project.

And so it was that our cult-information center was born. I was given a small office and a telephone line. In the previous years I had collected valuable information through my research. Data on most of the cults and new religious movements that were springing up rapidly in and around Britain had found a place in my files. With this background information, and a strong desire to help those in need, I was ready.

As demands for further information came my way, I expanded my research library. I contacted international agencies and help-groups that were involved in similar projects. We worked closely with researchers in America, Australia, Hong Kong, Japan, and Europe.

Eventually a number of us formed an informal international liaison of concerned groups. We pooled our research, coordinated strategies, and met on a regular basis to exchange advice. We spread news of our work through regular newsletters, concerned churches, educational facilities, and the media.

I was flooded with inquiries from overseas as well as Britain. People were desperately seeking information. One cult or another had lured their children, grandchildren, or friends into its net. They wanted someone to talk to. These Westerners couldn't begin to understand the Eastern guru system that often imposed a strange hold over their family members. They longed for advice on how to deal with the predicament of their estrangement.

Ghastly and tragic stories were reported to me. There were tales of manipulative persuasion resulting in physical, emotional, and spiritual imprisonment. Well-educated, middle- and upper-middle-class people were being entrapped. At times, those ensnared were children under the legal age of consent. During some weeks I reached the point of sheer exhaustion in trying to deal with as many as 250 personal inquiries.

As the media and government officials learned of the antisocial behavior within the cults, my work became more pressured. To ease the tension, I started up volunteer parent and aid groups to help with much of the counseling. We became a source of information for the media. They in turn energetically circulated the shocking information received from brokenhearted parents. I found myself being quoted in the world press and becoming a frequent guest on numerous radio and television shows. I was given the opportunity to speak before select members of the British House of Lords and House of Commons.

In December 1979, cult leader of the People's Temple, Jim Jones, ordered 913 of his devoted disciples to commit suicide. After this shocking news from Jonestown, Guyana, frightened members of other cults ran away from their groups. On coming out, they revealed unbelievable secrets of cruelties similar to those performed in Jonestown. Electric shocks, beatings, and assaults were common stories.

Disciples of other cults were driven to suicide because they were unable to meet the demands or humiliations of their group. The reports of cruelty often reminded me of the horrors of Hitler's concentration camps. We heard of the sterilization of women and young children. Abortions were ordered by one guru's hierarchy. Illegal smuggling of drugs and arms were carried out to raise money for other guru organizations.

Cults worldwide seemed to be nurturing mad paranoia. Public pressure forced investigations into ex-members' claims. In response, some cults ordered security guards armed with guns to protect them and their religious communities. Many of them spoke of forming their own city, much like Jim Jones had done.

My daily mail was piled high, not only with sad letters but worldwide press clippings commenting on cultic behavior and tactics and the public's reactions. Even prostitution and homosexual behavior were encouraged by various cults to entice outsiders into their groups. Children were being used as sexual bait too!

The seduction of new recruits is not the only important requirement in many cults. Devotees must also bring money as part of their spiritual offering. Under pressure, many cult members will do anything to bring in the "necessary" funds. They have come to believe that *the end justifies the means*—and their cause is the only reality.

Almost daily we heard of fraudulent methods used to elicit funds; we alerted the police, the public, and tax departments to be on the lookout. Money was being extracted from the unsuspecting public at airports, street corners, zoos, educational campuses, office buildings, and other public places. Supposedly the money would be used for charitable causes, such as drug rehabilitation and famine relief. But this was clearly not the case.

As individual cult members were driven by fanatical religious zeal to raise thousands of dollars daily, monumental cash stashes resulted. These funds put many cults into a competitive position when it came to purchasing extravagant amounts of real estate. Substantial bribes influenced businessmen and politicians on the gurus' behalf.

As the public began to be informed, methods of recruiting disciples, collecting funds, and propagating god-consciousness became more sophisticated. Front groups were often established, calling themselves by different names to avoid recognition.

My office was inundated with inquiries about the names of business enterprises that various cults operate, from health food stores to candle-making businesses, from poster to tee-shirt manufacturing. The businesses looked harmless and the projects seemed enterprising and commendable.

The sad fact is that governments and taxpayers worldwide are being robbed. The cults shelter their financial empires and businesses by enlisting them as religious, nonprofit charities. These complex structures are exempt from ordinary financial reporting. They are able to claim maximum tax benefits. To make matters worse, the cults supply their own workers (it is often slave labor, or at any rate cheap labor), enabling them to undercut legitimate businesses that are unable to compete.

We received complaints from entire villages in England. After a supposedly passive religious group moved into a local vicinity, villagers were intimidated, harassed, and sued. They were persecuted for not accepting the cult's antisocial behavior, philosophies, or ethics. Local industries and family businesses that had flourished for years were undercut by the new residents.

The more literature I read, and the more information I received on the various cult conglomerates, the more I began to see a familiar pattern: financial greed, hunger for power, and authoritarian leaders. It was no surprise to see global political power becoming the goal of many cults.

Probably the most common complaints I heard regarded the way cults distributed their teachings. Eastern and occultic philosophies were offered in educational centers, recreational centers, military establishments, and success and business management seminars. This was happening without the full knowledge of the participants.

In some cases, the message came disguised in scientific and psychological packaging. This was especially true with TM and Yoga. Very seldom did cults or human potential groups openly acknowledge their religious status. Neither did they admit to potential psychological or spiritual dangers.

I once got into a conversation with a couple of members of a large, well-known sect outside a little shop they owned. They stopped me, supposedly to take information for some sort of market survey. "What time of day do you normally shop?" they began. Before long, however, I was led to personal, emotional questions. Then it was suggested that I take a free psychological test at their headquarters.

Besides these ploys, cults also use marriage and employment counseling for recruitment. Needy, unsuspecting people are lured into the group while seeking help from an agency they believe is neutral.

The most tragic stories, however, had to do with India—my childhood's homeland. Sons, daughters, grandchildren, even parents were disappearing while seeking spiritual answers in India. I had a list of missing cult members that grew longer every month. A letter from a Swedish friend added to my sense of alarm:

> Many young people have gone to India looking for spiritual enlightenment. Instead they've found despair and death . . . 1½ million of them suffer from drug addiction, starvation, horrible brutalities, and utter hopelessness. There are many murders, many suicides, and thousands of deaths by disease and starvation.

I had a growing feeling that I would soon have to go back to India myself. Fluency in Indian languages and familiarity with the country gave me the right credentials. I needed to search for those lost people whose relatives had come to me for help. And in the process I would hear firsthand what the gurus, *the gods of the New Age*, were really teaching.

Taj Mahal

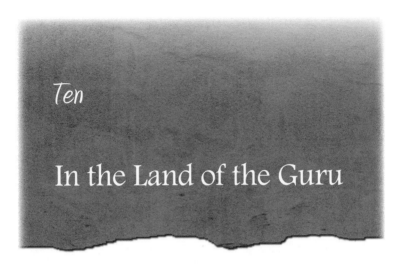

Ten

In the Land of the Guru

Thirteen years had passed since my family had left India. Now I found myself on an airplane returning there. I was filled with excitement and nostalgic memories. Would I bump into old friends with whom I had lost contact over the years? Would anything have changed?

I was travelling with a small group of international cult experts. We had received a grant enabling our research group to travel around India, visiting gurus and their *ashrams.**

In between our work, we planned to see some of the marvels of India. There was no doubt in my mind that India's world-famous tourist attractions would be as intriguing as ever I remembered them.

During our flight, I thumbed through the colorful travel booklet in the seat pocket. The Taj Mahal of Agra, just outside Delhi, India's capital, still looked magnificent. This monumental tomb immortalizes a touching love story. It is exquisitely beautiful,

---

*Ashrams: In India, a place of religious retreat for Hindus

built in perfect symmetry with translucent white marble. It is also a grand tribute to the craftsmen who created its interior. The Taj Mahal has always reminded me of the maharajas' palaces. They, too, reflect days of bygone splendor, and stand out in arrogant contrast to the surrounding poverty.

Another spectacular sight we planned to see was the golden temple of the Sikhs at Amritsar. Located in the state of Punjab, it is the *Mecca* of the Sikh religion.

Marketplace in Delhi

Calcutta

Our plane landed in Calcutta, the former capital of the British Indian Empire and the city of my birth—I was breathless with excitement. Yet my enthusiasm was tinged with fear and apprehension: I knew the India I would encounter over the next few weeks would be a very different India from that of my youth.

This time I would experience the hardships of living an ascetic life with gurus and their disciples, a lifestyle as foreign to me as it was to my companions.

We planned to examine various popular-in-the-West gurus. We would interview them as well as their disciples, trying to glean a basic understanding of their teachings, so that we could better educate our various organizations back home. We also hoped to return annually to update our findings.

I anticipated hardships, knowing that many gurus hid themselves in the outbacks of India's countryside. I knew that the diets and accompanying Hindu religious activities would be arduous and draining. If all this weren't spiritually exhausting, it would definitely take its toll physically.

The Mirrored Temple, center of Jain worship in Calcutta, India

Any disappointments I expected certainly didn't match up to the overwhelming reality, which I soon encountered. Calcutta is named after the frightful Hindu goddess Kali, the female counterpart of the male god Shiva. Both depict death and destruction, and the city clearly reflects this. Kali also has the benign title of Mother of Love. Calcutta, or Kali-ghat, "the steps to Kali," embodies all the complex contradictions of the Hindu god-goddess makeup. Calcutta is also one of the biggest cities in the world, with a population of nearly thirteen million. Its harbors and industries make it a key center of Eastern commerce.

The first thing to overwhelm me as I stepped into Dum Dum, the bustling Calcutta airport, was the wild confusion resulting from overpopulation. Being in the midst of shoulder-to-shoulder people was a sensation I had almost forgotten after spending years in the West.

I recalled a conversation with an Indian friend who had visited America. He had commented on the emptiness of American streets. "Where are all the people?" he had asked in bewilderment. "I see houses with cars parked outside, open shops, offices, and restaurants . . . but where are all the people?" That question might seem peculiar to those who have not experienced India's swarming mass of humanity.

My thoughts were soon flooded with other unpleasant recollections. Besides the pushing and shoving, we had to deal with stealing and lying—almost-forgotten aspects of my childhood memories.

Upon swift recall of necessary survival instincts, I made immediate efforts to beat the corruption of "the system." Unfortunately, I wasn't fast enough to protect our little group from the first "criminal."

One of our party was taken in by a fellow claiming to be a porter. Our naïve traveling companion had paid an up-front deposit. Without hesitation, the imposter had proceeded to put our collective baggage onto a trolley. He had then wheeled it off down the road toward points unknown.

Because I was fluent in Hindi, I was assigned the recovery operation. Eventually, I caught up to the thief and ordered him to return our baggage to the airport lobby. He did so, but, of course, we lost the deposit. He stubbornly claimed it had not been paid to him. After this incident, I quickly learned to stay on my toes.

The next minor incident (our last show of naiveté) was a deliberately elongated taxi drive from the airport. Since I vaguely remembered the surroundings enough to put our cab driver back on course, we were spared the expense of being driven around and around the city. But, oh, the streets of Calcutta we drove through. Pitiful shacks made up of sackcloth, rags, and sticks engulfed the sidewalks and spilled onto the streets.

When our cab stopped for a moment at a traffic light, I was able to peek into the dark interiors of some of those "homes." I was still horrified, after all the years, to see the number of people living inside. Sisters and brothers were curled against each other like young gerbils in a cage. I saw one pathetically skinny child in tattered rags with cow-dung matted in her hair. She was attempting to soothe a wailing toddler. She cuddled and caressed him, with a comforting smile on her sweet, sad face.

How could the Western spiritual seekers I had spoken to in England, Europe, and America overlook so much tragedy? How could they bypass it to focus on the "wisdom and love" of the East? Couldn't they see that it was the very aloofness and madness of India's religion, her so-called wisdom and love, that created such obvious agony for the poor and such cruel apathy in the rich?

They had only to look at any of the ever-present beggars. As a member of one of the largest professions there, each beggar belongs to a master. He is assigned to a specific territory where he collects money for his owner. In return, he is provided with a cramped space in some hovel for sleeping and an occasional meager meal.

Some of these homeless derelicts are horribly diseased. Others are intentionally mutilated by their masters. Some children are

maimed from birth in order to elicit sympathy from prospective donors.
Equally heartbreaking are India's prostitutes. According to one government-commissioned study, there are three million prostitutes in India, with many of them between the ages of twelve and fifteen.[1] Young girls are often recruited by pimps who tour rural villages, making wild financial promises to poverty-stricken parents. Male prostitution in India is on the rise too.

In Mumbai, there is an infamous street where young girls are kept behind iron bars. Cage after cage exposes scantily clad, heavily made-up teenagers. Some are extraordinarily beautiful. Others are barely ten years old. Many have been beaten and tortured into submission.[2]

How does the higher class Indian deal with all this cultural madness? With sure escape in mind, he does what any Westerner might do when stressed—he goes to the movies!

India has the largest film industry in the world, far surpassing the number of films made in the United States, and there are over 13,000 theaters. Every three months a billion people in India buy tickets to the cinema.[3] Even in the poorest regions of the country, people would go short of food rather than give up their night with the movie stars.

In an impoverished, starving country some films cost their producers tens of millions of rupees. The controversial 1981 film, *Gandhi*, was all the rage in fashionable Indian circles. One-third of the film's nine million pound (English sterling) budget was paid for by the Indian government.[4] Such were India's political priorities.

Meanwhile, alluring tourist propaganda puts out impressive statistics documenting India's achievements. But these glowing reports fail to address the nation's most sobering problems.

India is the seventh largest landmass in the world. Her population of over 1.1 billion makes her the second most inhabited country on earth.[5]

Yet, in spite of her size, a spectacular array of natural resources, and economic growth due to developing technological industries, India places twelfth among the economies of the world.[6] And although India is rising economically, malnutrition, lack of educational opportunity, and overall poverty is still extremely high: nearly half of India's children are underweight for their age;[7] there are seventeen million child laborers in India; less than half of India's children between the ages of six and fourteen go to school; more than one in three women in India and over sixty percent of the children in India are anemic.[8]

Ashrams of India

The first ashram our group visited was the Sivananda Ashram in Monghyr. Also known as the Bihar School of Yoga, it was founded in 1964 by Tantric Swami Satyananda Saraswati. When we arrived there, the powers-that-be required that we pay the exorbitant overnight accommodation fees in advance. We consented. We were tired and hungry and didn't have the energy to complain over the high costs. We had had an exhausting overnight train journey from

A train at rest at a remote hill station in India

Calcutta. Jamalpur Junction, the train station nearest the ashram, was located six miles away. To make matters worse, we had arrived in the wee hours of the morning.

The station guard had warned us not to venture out of the station. "You'll be robbed or murdered!" he had declared. He said that the State of Bihar was one of the most violent in all of India. Our kind friend felt that it would be wiser if we stayed on the station platform until dawn. We did so, along with hundreds of other passengers.

Tired, but grateful for the sage advice, we settled down for a long night's vigil. The gangways were festooned with sleeping bodies and the debris of luggage. The only place we could find to sit in was the filthy, dimly lit station restaurant. This was a far cry from the crisply clean and hygienic eating houses of my childhood that I recalled so vividly.

A waiter appeared, wearing the same uniform of three decades past. It looked as though it hadn't been laundered for almost that long! His faded red turban and cummerbund sadly reflected years of deterioration. It was barely discernible that his gray, permanently stained tunic had once been white. His gloves, once a colonial symbol of cleanliness, were almost too filthy to look at; the frayed seams at his fingertips exposed grease-stained nails.

I looked up into his face. "How many years have you been working for the railroad?" I asked him in Hindi. "Since I was a child," he smiled proudly. "Since the time of the British Raj." His eyes looked back into the past, and filled with sorrow at the reminiscence. "Things have changed a lot." He looked around him, waving his arm slowly as if pointing out something. He glanced at the bedraggled uniform that he still wore with an element of pride, and shrugged. "Things have changed," he repeated. Then he sighed and smiled in weary resignation, "What would you like to order, Mehemsahib?" His tiny, blunt pencil was poised above a pad that had been written on over and over again.

As dawn brightened the skyline, we collected our small bundles of luggage and hailed a rickshaw-puller. He took us a mile or so short of the Sivananda community. We walked the rest of the way.

The accommodations at the ashram were sparse; the spiritual tasks were arduous. All the disciples were Westerners who had to work hard for their keep. They did the most menial chores—cleaning lavatories, peeling vegetables, sweeping floors. All the jobs that my family's untouchable servants had done in my youth were done by the residents there. Any Indians present were presumably the guru's aides. They held "higher" responsibilities. The Westerners regarded their work as religious service. This fell under the category of Karma Yoga, the Yoga of "selfless labor" performed for the sake of "spiritual evolution."

I slept in a large dormitory with about ten other girls. We were awakened at 4:00 a.m. each morning; some of the disciples gathered in meditation classes, while others involved themselves in private practice. On our first morning, the girl in the rope bed next to me woke me up. Her quiet alarm clock had sounded, making her sit bolt-upright. She then pulled her blanket over her head. She was getting herself poised in a lotus position, ready for her own brand of Yoga.

The girl sat still for quite some time, long enough for me to get comfortable and doze off to sleep again. Then she started an uncanny humming, low and monotonous. She hardly seemed to breathe in at all. She just kept blowing out one long, scary tone. It sent goose bumps up and down me. At last I could stand it no longer. I got up and watched the morning activities in the rest of the ashram.

There were those who practiced *neti*, the cleansing of the nose with warm salted water. The small container used could hold up to two cups of water and had a long spout. It looked rather like a strange teapot. The spout was shoved up the nostril. (It looked most uncomfortable to me.) The devotee breathed in and out, sneezing, choking, coughing.

Neti is said to cleanse the membranes inside the nose and to stimulate and strengthen the surrounding area, which includes the eyebrow center. To Hindus this is an important contact point for the *anja chakra*—the third eye.

Physical perversions are aspects of Kriya Yoga—the type Gandhi practiced. Perhaps it was part of the madness that had led him to administer enemas to his favorite female devotees. His weird sexual quirks had had him sleeping with nude teenage girls in an attempt to confirm his celibacy. And his extraordinary perspectives on fitness caused him to prescribe cow-dung pills for health![9]

Gandhi had been a guru with his own ashram long before he became a political figure. Like a score of other god-men, he had believed that Kriya Yoga balances the psychic energies and awakens the chakras.

A young Australian girl sat next to a neti disciple as I spoke with him. Later that night she paid me an unexpected visit. Perched on a log with my rationed half-bucket of water, I was contemplating how to wash my face, teeth, hair, and underwear. *Can I accomplish such a feat?* I was wondering when I heard the cracking of a twig nearby. In a few seconds, I saw someone hesitantly come out of the shadows.

I recognized the girl and warmly asked her to join me. She did. There was probably about a minute of silence. Then she gathered up enough courage to say shyly, "You seem as though you have come from another planet. You've got such a warm and friendly glow of color all around you."

I had learned not to laugh at such statements. I dipped my washcloth into the bucket and started wiping my face.

"You've got a different kind of life in you. Where are you from?" she questioned. We ended up talking for a couple of hours, until regulations caused the ashram to fall silent at 9:00 p.m.

I learned that Premananda was only twenty-one. She had been a disciple of Satyananda for five years, recruited while still at school. There are numerous branches of this guru's ashram in many different countries. *How quickly the different schools of Yoga are growing all over the world*, I thought. That very morning I had read a large sign there at the ashram that said: "Yoga will emerge as a mighty world power and will change the course of world events."[10]

"Do you practice all the methods of Kriya Yoga, such as

Amoroli?" I asked the young girl. By that time, she trusted me.

"Well, I'm meant to do it," she said apologetically. "But it tastes so terrible that it makes me feel sick."

Poor girl, I thought. What a ghastly spiritual duty. Those poor devotees had to drink urine as part of their Yogic discipline. They had been taught that it contained redemptive qualities.

"Do you know what urine really is?" She shook her head. "Well," I tried to explain, "it's the body's waste product. There's nothing in it that the body needs anymore. So of course it makes you feel sick. And how can it possibly save you?"

Premananda went on to confide that one of her friends had been told to drink her guru's urine. "I wouldn't know what to do if that were to happen to me!" Her eyes grew wide at the prospect.

My research had shown that it was believed anything that touched the body of a guru was holy, from the dust of his feet to his dirty dishes. Drinking a guru's bathwater is said to be enlightening. Should the guru desire sex, the disciple (whether male or female) is to look upon the act as a step up his spiritual ladder. So I knew that drinking the guru's urine was a devotional duty of great significance.

All these specifics are spelled out in the Guru-gita, a Hindu scripture. "Meditate ceaselessly on the form of the Guru," this ancient document commands. It also states:

> [A]lways repeat his name, carry out his orders, think
> not of anything except the Guru. . . . Through service
> at the feet of the Guru the embodied soul becomes
> purified and all its sins are washed away.[11]

After a few days, we moved on to the next ashram, leaving behind many spiritual prisoners. I couldn't help but pray for those poor victims. I also thanked God for the opportunity to speak to a handful of them. Some of the followers were closed, like the neti disciple. Others were open, like Premananda. Her guru, Satyananda, had demanded that his devotees cut themselves off from the outside world, but I had been able to encourage her to get in touch with her parents. I was able to activate her conscience regarding the rights and wrongs of some of her practices. Perhaps it would help her reconsider her commitment to a god of India.

Orthodox Hinduism teaches four stages of life: the learning stage of childhood, the stage of marital responsibilities, the stage of career obligations, and the stage of spiritual preparation for death. The Yoga disciplines teach how to cease the body's functions, in preparation for death, or as Hindus believe, to enter into reincarnation. The traditional purpose of the Indian ashram had always been to teach people how to die through Yoga meditation.

West Goes East

It was only after the 1960s that young Westerners, inspired by the Beatles, began to flood India's ashrams to sit spellbound at the feet of gurus. Initially, they used India's spiritual communities as hostels. They provided cheap accommodations for the young seekers while they explored their mystical whims.

By the 1980s, their presence had changed the traditional atmosphere at many ashrams. Along with the youthful Westerners came children and a more family-oriented environment. The influx of Westerners also altered the ashrams' structure: new requirements for ashram life and the practice of Yoga bypassed the ancient Brahmin qualifications; regardless of sex, nationality, caste, or creed, everyone was accepted. And what was once only available to elderly Hindus became available to all.

Although ashrams have been made available to outsiders, the message of the gurus and the purpose of Yoga remain unchanged. People in the West have been deceived into thinking it is the art of living; but to people in the East, it is the art of dying.

Many of the Western converts to Yoga have helped spread it in the West. One Westerner who spent time in a Hindu ashram and has had significant influence upon the Western world is Michael Ray, a Stanford University professor. Ray created the "Creativity in Business" course, which takes "much of its inspiration from Eastern philosophies, mysticism, and meditation techniques."[12] Ray describes his ashram experience:

I attended a meditation-intensive day at an ashram to support a friend. As I sat in meditation in what was for me an unfamiliar environment, I suddenly felt and saw a bolt of lightning shoot up from the base of my spine out the top of my head. It forced me to recognize something great within me . . . this awareness of my own divinity.[13]

Ray now tells his students they can get in touch with their "inner person" or "spirit-guide," who will guide them through life.[14] Since his visit to an ashram, Ray has passed on his Eastern wisdom to thousands through books and seminars.

Even Christianity has been indirectly affected by Ray. In 1982, Jim Collins, a speaker at Christian conferences, took Ray's course, "Creativity in Business." He was so inspired by the course that he wrote the foreword for Ray's 2004 book *The Highest Goal*. Collins says he discovered "the path to my highest goal" by reading the book. What is this highest goal that Michael Ray speaks of? His "own divinity." In *The Highest Goal*, Ray speaks openly about Eastern meditation techniques and quotes Hindu gurus such as Ram Dass, Jiddu Krishnamurti, and Swami Shantananda.

Silence: The Only True Religion?

The influence of Eastern thinking and Yoga upon the West continues in many forms. In October 2007, television talk-show host Oprah Winfrey introduced fifty million viewers to a book titled, *Eat, Pray, Love*. The book, written by Elizabeth Gilbert, recounts how she left her husband and former way of life and found what she came to call the only true religion: the silence. Her journey took her around the world, and finally to India where she learned to meditate in an ashram.

Gilbert explained that the first step in her journey was to go on an eating binge in Italy:

I would not have been able to physically do the Yoga, the meditation, the hard rigor of spiritual work. So

I went to Italy first and I ate my guts out for four months.[15]

From Italy, Gilbert traveled to India where she learned to meditate:

There was something about that Yoga path that really appealed to me—and you do that through silence and the discipline of meditation—and I really wanted to go pursue that full out.

None of this works without stillness . . . One of the great teachings that I learned in India is that silence is the only true religion.[16]

During her time at the ashram, Gilbert had a meditative experience in which she says, "the scales fell from my eyes and the openings of the universe were shown to me."[17]

Interestingly, Gilbert related a story of how a newfound meditating friend experienced "colors," "sounds," "whirling," and "twirling" during his meditation times.[18] This is a description of the *kundalini* (meaning serpent power in Hinduism) *effect* experienced by Yoga practitioners. Kundalini is said to be lying dormant, coiled at the base of the spine. When it is awakened and encouraged up the spinal passage it ultimately achieves cosmic union with the third eye. The serpent's journey passes through 'chakras' or psychic centers. And mystical powers are aroused as it progresses. A similar experience led to mystic and Catholic priest Philip St. Romain hearing the voices of other beings, which he called his "inner adviser[s]."[19]

Eat, Pray, Love has been on the *New York Times* Best Sellers List since its release and has sold over five million copies thus far. Sadly, a popular Christian writer and speaker, Anne Lamott, wrote an endorsement for the book, which sits on the back cover. Lamott is best known for her own book, *Traveling Mercies.* Of *Eat, Pray, Love* she says: "This is a wonderful book, brilliant and personal, rich in spiritual insight."[20] But the "spiritual insight" from Gilbert's book is the same "insight" the Hindu gurus teaching Yoga in India have been passing along to the masses for centuries. The aim of all Hinduism is to escape the hopeless cycle of reincarnation, wherein the soul passes on from body to soul, to body to soul, over and over again. The purpose of Yoga is to prepare a person to cut off the relationship between himself and the physical world, in preparation for death. He is trained to stop his life processes, to stop thinking, to stop the senses, to stop breathing. Hindus believe the escape from all this living and dying is through Yoga.

Returning to India after thirteen years as a Christian on a research team, I was able to recognize how complicated and con-tradictory the philosophy of Hinduism really is. Through Yoga, the practitioner trains himself to slow down and eventually stop his life processes. Even the breathing exercises taught in Yoga are not intended to be a health benefit. They are not designed to en-able one to breathe more efficiently, but to control one's breath-ing. The purpose is to enable one to slow the breathing down to a minimum in order to stop it one day altogether. Yoga's *gift* is merely a form of suicide.

In contrast, Jesus said He came to give those who follow Him life. He is the antithesis of death—His resurrection is a powerful illustration of this:

> I am the resurrection, and the life: he that believeth in me, though he were dead, yet shall he live: And whosoever liveth and believeth in me shall never die. (John 11: 25,26)

Festivals
in INDIA

Indian ladies dressed in brightly colored sari's watching
games at a festival in India

Eleven

Two Aquarian Fairs— East and West

The bus I was riding in India with my research team had quietly come to a stop. In the course of our expedition, we had visited a total of sixteen ashrams. Sometimes we were welcomed. Sometimes we were shunned.

We gathered our belongings and stepped into the dusty street. The final adventure in our arduous Indian journey was about to begin.

Expectantly, we walked together to the crest of a little hill. A faint breeze stirred the warm air. Suddenly, there before us, a glorious sunset blazed orange fire across the merging Ganges and Jamnu rivers. Below us sat the Kumbh-Mela festival, spread lavishly over acres and acres of land. Festival trappings extended as far as the eye could see, with thousands of tents methodically laid out in parallel rows. Brilliantly hued canopies proclaimed the presence of several hundred participating gurus. Around each guru temporary ashrams had been erected—compact individual "cities," each with its own water and power supply. These were regularly interspersed among the tents.

Kumbh-Mela

The Kumbh-Mela festival takes place every fourteen years, when it is believed that certain planets and stars and all the astrological energies are fixed in the right places. Millions of Indians gather for this religious festival. The people come together for a vortex of energy, a kind of spiritual zap, some walking hundreds of miles to get there. The event lasts for a month.

Making our way down into the midst of the celebrants, we began to explore along the dirt streets that separated the temporary dwellings, where thousands of vendors displayed their colorful wares. Mounds of yellow, red, and fluorescent pink dyes were for sale. These would be used for ceremonial staining of the gurus' and devotees' clothing.

Myriad sacred necklaces of various lengths, fashioned of wooden beads, nuts, and seeds, hung in display. For a price, one could also acquire an idol of one's favorite god, or purchase a vessel of any size with which to carry holy Ganges water back home. Fruits and vegetables for the satisfaction of hungry pilgrims were artistically displayed

A flamboyantly decorated elephant plodded past us, raising clouds of dust. His guru and *mahoot* (trainer) were on his back. They were collecting alms and food.

A hungry cow loitered outside an ashram. Soon a conscientious Hindu ran to its aid, believing he furthered his own salvation by providing a bowl of rice for the skinny beast.

We hardly said a word to each other as we struggled through the throngs. The noise around us was deafening. Each ashram amplified the announcement of its program, and the sounds mingled chaotically with all the others. Ear-splitting sound levels promoted various spiritual shows. Religious songs were performed. Spiritual messages were broadcast.

As we passed the various gurus' ashrams, we observed that *satsangs* and *darshans* (religious monologues) were being offered to the pilgrims who crammed themselves into the crowded tents.

Women were segregated from men, while the guru sat alone on a decorated stage. Money, fruit, and flowers rested at his feet—offerings from the faithful. Women reverently moved to the front and bowed before him, touching and kissing his feet.

Beggars lined the busy thoroughfares. Loudspeakers warned the public of thieves and pickpockets, announced the whereabouts of lost children, and gave notice of forthcoming programs.

The Western devotees of Hare Krishna looked strangely out of place in this obviously Hindu atmosphere. Nevertheless, they chanted and wailed "Hare Krishna" through their loudspeakers. And above their heads they bore a carefully mounted picture of their dead guru.

Astrologers sold their skills everywhere we turned. Astrology, of course, is a widespread Hindu practice. Indian business dealings can often take months to accomplish because many business owners wait on corporate astrologers to determine the most auspicious days to make certain transactions. No matter how trivial the personal decision, it cannot be made without the Hindu consulting his personal stargazers. Major decisions regarding such matters as marriage, child-bearing, building homes, or changing careers require the most careful and meticulous astrological consideration.

At one point, we saw that an "electronic" astrology reading was available. A board displaying zodiac signs was propped on a bicycle. If we put coins in the odd-looking machine and listened through some very grubby-looking headphones, we could hear our horoscopes. What advanced technology!

For further information about the future, one fellow had trained a forecasting parrot. When money was presented to the man, the parrot popped out of his cage and selected a playing card from a deck, which was laid out face-down in the dirt. The bright-green bird then returned to his cage, and the fortune-teller proceeded to interpret the card's meaning. Palm-readers also collected coins as they read the handprints of anxious pilgrims.

Nearby, a snake-charmer coaxed his reptilian business partner into action with a haunting, piped melody. It is difficult to escape the presence of serpents at a Hindu festival. In fact, the symbol of the snake has appeared in all cultures throughout the ages. It always accompanies the practice of mystical and occultic rituals.

Here and there we encountered Yogis doing various acts of violence to themselves. This was a means of proving that they could control their Yoga-induced altered states.

Over the years, I have seen horrible examples of this kind of fanaticism. Some individuals hang themselves for days by hundreds of hooks attached to their skin, their tongues, or their private parts. Others lie on beds of long rusty nails or barbed wire. One guru stood without lying or sitting for a supposed thirty-eight-year period, much of the time in water. (He had the most ghastly varicose veins.)

There at the festival, a large crowd gathered around a group of naked priests who looked half-crazed. They were obviously heavily drugged. The ground in front of them had been dug to make a large hole and lined with white-hot rocks. It looked like a fiery grave. Drums beat rhythmically and endlessly. One by one the nude, ash-smeared holy men danced in a hypnotic trance back and forth across the searing stones.

The Yoga of Suffering

Self-mortifying acts as described above fall into the category of *tapas*. This is an integral part of Hinduism's contradictory focus on suffering. Whether physical, emotional, or spiritual suffering is involved, Eastern philosophy says that since the world as we see it is unreal, suffering doesn't really exist; we are blind to the immortal nature and too aware of the mortal.

This means that we must transcend the body. In doing so, we can disconnect ourselves from physical pain. Through Yoga we can use our minds to develop willpower, to raise our focus, to concentrate and move ourselves out of the physical, up to the mental, and eventually into the spiritual.

The Yoga of suffering was endorsed by Maharishi Mahesh Yogi of Transcendental Meditation. His ashram was in full view at the Kumbh-Mela. He was heard to say:

The hungry man can be a happy hungry man if he meditates. Begin to look inward, wherein lies the kingdom of heaven. When the Self is realized, all pain and suffering vanish; suffering is retardation—going downward in evolution. Suffering is the result of sin. And meditation is the way to close the gate.[1]

In another ashram I heard of Prabhupada, the now-deceased guru of the Hare Krishnas, who once said:

If someone is not getting any good, that is a blessing. It is God's arrangement to correct him . . . The so-called starvation problem is just a mental concoction. . . . Each man's suffering is simply his own fault.[2]

Thus, the hopeless future for the Hindu is a promise of suffering again and again through reincarnation.

This is completely opposite to the message of Christianity where God has taken upon Himself human suffering through the Cross of Jesus Christ in order to redeem all who come to Him by faith through grace. Salvation is a gift that no man can earn—God offers it freely. Jesus' suffering for us on the Cross, and paying the penalty for our sins, is the basis of the Christian faith, and it is in stark contrast to Hinduism.

The Yoga of suffering, futile as it is, is one of the eight recognized Yoga techniques or "paths." However, the gurus combine many of them into their own peculiar brand of salvation. They then market their personal concoctions to the West as stress-reducing, mind-calming programs. Despite its Western packaging, however, Yoga cannot be considered without its spiritual ramifications.

I listened to one Kumbh-Mela guru explaining Yoga to his rapt audience: "Our physical bodies with their constant demands for food, sleep, and other 'earthly' wants must be controlled. Once the physical is mastered, spiritual heights can be achieved."

Among the Yogas I saw offered at the Kumbh-Mela were Hatha Yoga, the one most familiar in the West. This Yoga requires strict breath control and incorporates *asanas* or positions. The familiar cross-legged Yoga position called the *Lotus* and the handstand are Hatha Yoga asanas. We also saw Bhakti Yoga, the Yoga of devotion, which the Hare Krishnas practice. A group called the Brahma Kumaris offered Raja Yoga—the "royal" path to enlightenment. The Divine Light Mission promoted Light-and-Sound Yoga, with its *third-eye* initiation. White Tantra and Kundalini Yoga were evident everywhere. Essentially, despite the different names and terminology, all are the same Hindu concept of God.

Politics and Religion—Indian Style

Despite all the mystical madness of Hinduism, the Kumbh-Mela festival is government sponsored. The reason for this is that India's politics and religion are inseparably entwined. Certain radical nationalistic political parties are deeply involved with and sponsored by the Hindu group, Vishwa Hindu Parishad (VHP, meaning World Hindu Council). The World Hindu Council is dedicated to the worldwide spread of Hinduism. On their website, it states that the VHP objective is to "organise-consolidate the Hindu society and to serve-protect the Hindu Dharma . . . [with] a strong and self confident Hindu organisation . . . taking shape."[3]

To this end, the VHP conducts many conferences both inside and outside of India, such as the large, international mission conferences in connection with the huge Kumbh-Mela.

At the time that we attended the Kumbh-Mela in the 1980s, the VHP was still a secret organization; Indians would claim no knowledge of it to outsiders. However, while we'd waited in a dusty little town until it was time for the bus to depart for the Kumbh-Mela, members of our group "accidentally" stumbled upon a trove of literature published by the VHP stating its mission and stratagems to convert the world to Hinduism. The VHP-sponsored Rashtriya Swayam Sevak, or the RSS, was the strongest religious-political movement we saw represented at that Kumbh-Mela festival. The RSS has one major goal—to establish a pure state of Hinduism within India. The party is strongly anti-Muslim and anti-Christian.

Both of these religions are considered to be foreign to Indians. Many times the RSS has demanded, while exerting cruel pressure, that Indians convert back to Hinduism. A statement made by the VHP indicates their commitment in this regard:

> By taking up . . . the religious conversions of Hindus by Christian Church . . . VHP is proving to be the indomitable force of the Hindu society for the protection of its core values-beliefs and sacred traditions.[4]

Since the 1980s, these militant nationalistic groups have gained political power and patronage and are so powerful that their members have influenced every part of Indian society. In 2006, the RSS initiated the passing of anti-conversion laws in four Indian states, making it a criminal offence to convert to Christianity for both the converter and converted. They have been responsible for the rise in the violent persecution of India's Christians.

The Ganges River

At the time of our visit to India, however, these groups were only beginning their rise to power.

The Indian government had spent millions to efficiently present the festival we were attending. There was an overabundance of facilities. The press was welcomed with superb accommodations, telephone lines, post office facilities, and free transportation. Hundreds of clerks and supervisors were allocated to look after the twenty million pilgrims. Police and fire-fighting equipment was strategically placed. Water was provided, as was electricity—to light the neon signs and power the roaring loudspeakers that surrounded every ashram.

All the preparations were geared toward the climax of the festival: the traditional bath in the Ganges River ceremonially taken by every pilgrim. The more influential priests and gurus lead an enormously lengthy parade to the river. An established order, based on hierarchical preference, determines who follows whom to the holy water's edge.

First come the highly reverenced *Nagas*, who are said to be serpent-embodied demigods. They are armed and naked, and they serve as honored guards for the gurus. Many of them appear to be totally insane.

Next come the guru entourages transporting the *god-men* in Indian-style luxury. Sometimes they appear in elaborate sedan chairs carried by struggling devotees. Others ride vividly painted elephants decked out in full regalia. Certain special gurus use mechanical vehicles—signifying great prestige.

Whatever his mode of transport, each guru is seen as super-human. He is an enlightened master. He has liberated himself from the consequences of karma. Thus, desperate pilgrims stand ecstatically in the dirt that their gurus have touched. They apply it to their faces and carry it home to their families. The very dust that a guru's entourage has passed through promises a glimmer of hope for eventual karmic "salvation."

Following the gurus in the procession come male devotees. Far behind them come the women, the widows, and the lower castes.

Daytime view of Varanasi in northern
India on the Ganges River

Eventually every one of the millions of people reaches the river.

The waters from *Mother Ganga* are held to possess all spiritual qualities. They are the source and support of spiritual life. They can destroy evil spirits and are used as a charm to repel them. The waters can create fertility when sprinkled on newlyweds. They can heal the sick. The river can send the dying victoriously into the journey beyond this life, so its water is poured into their mouths.

Sometimes dying people can be found lying in the Ganges waters literally for weeks, waiting to die there. Their hope is that dying in this auspicious place will shorten the pains of their afterlife.

The worship and reverence of the Ganges poses a sensitive political and environmental problem for the Indian government. The pollution of the Ganges, which has steadily increased over the last few decades, endangers the lives of millions of people who regard it as their primary source of water. Nearly 400 million people live in the Ganges basin.[5] But to declare the river polluted is tantamount to blasphemy!

Industrial waste dumped into the river is not the only problem; additional discharge includes human and animal bodies as well as human sewage. The foul-smelling green and brown waters serve as

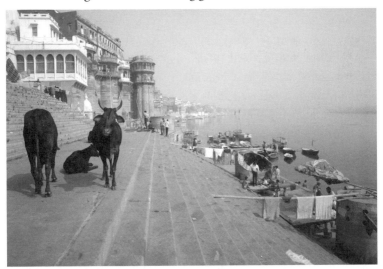

A scene from a town in India along the Ganges River

a urinal and public lavatory—as free floating feces testified. Even so, the river is used for washing laundry and for bathing humans and animals. It is also used for every kind of religious ceremony. Millions are drawn to its banks annually for spiritual reasons.[6]

During the waning hours of the Kumbh-Mela festival, I sat and gazed at the activities in and around the river. My eyes followed a young man in a rickety boat cruising toward some destination downstream. Due to the festival conducted on its shores, the river's waters were, if possible, more polluted than ever. But in spite of this, the young man reached his hand over the side of his little vessel, leaned out, and took a drink.

Hinduism, I thought as I watched him, *teaches man to seek for spiritual enlightenment within himself. Just like this poor soul, people are being poisoned while they try to satisfy their thirsty souls.*

Mind, Body, Spirit, in the UK

An uneventful journey home soon led me back to the whirlwind of my London job. Before long, impressions of the wild chaos of the Kumbh-Mela were lost in the work-a-day world, to resurface only as fleeting memories. It wasn't many weeks, however, before I found myself at an all-too-similar event; this time being held right in my own backyard.

"Mind Body Spirit Festival" the brochure read at Olympia Exhibition Hall in West London. I walked to the local underground station and waited for the next tube to Hammersmith. The familiar rumbling and gust of tunnel air told me the train was arriving. The doors slid open. I took my seat and began the dark ride. The Aquarian Fair lay at the end of my journey.

The annual festival, which began in 1977 and is still taking place today in major cities around the world, attracts thousands of people each year. This first festival was organized by the Unity-in-Diversity Council. As I sat on the train heading for the festival, I read some promotional material about this Council. It stated that, at the inspiration of the United Nations, six organizations came together with the common vision of seeing:

> . . . a worldwide body of individuals, groups and
> networks [which would] foster realization of the Source
> of All Life and of the unified nature of humanity
> and facilitate personal and social transformation and
> cooperative activities for global peace.[7]

I knew from other research that the Unity-In-Diversity Council had linked arms with the Mind, Body and Spirit festivals. This
formed a vast army dedicated to the merger of all religions into
one, under a world leader.

The train stopped, and I hurried out before the doors closed. I
rode an escalator up until I could see daylight ahead. A long walk
took me on to Olympia Hall and a day of New Age revelation.

I bought my festival ticket at the booth outside. Walking into
the huge auditorium, I was immediately overwhelmed by a carnival
atmosphere. Strange music was resounding throughout the place.
The first stand I came to was for macrobiotic food, complete with
explanatory brochures. Even in my vegetarian days I hadn't committed myself to anything so extreme as this. Macrobiotic eaters
believe that foods must not only be vegetarian, but they must be
grown in certain places and eaten only in certain combinations.
Flavor and texture, judging by what I sampled there, are definitely
a not top priority to this regimen.

Once the shock of seeing so many things at once began to wear
off, I began to understand what was being offered. Colorful posters
and beautiful displays offered quartz crystals. These are used for
meditation, and their use is said to provide healing energy.

Another little alcove touted color analysis. I knew from my
days of psychic awareness that everyone supposedly has a colorful aura, but I had never mastered the *coding* that enables people
to judge the character and mood of those around them. Color
analysis bears some similarity to the study of the zodiac.

Like the Kumbh-Mela, this Aquarian Fair also provided opportunities for individuals to have their horoscopes analyzed—
where anyone could learn of his future as well as his strengths
and weaknesses at the horoscope booth. One Westernized Hindu,

Swami Sivananda (an American, born in Philadelphia), declared astrology to be the religion of the Aquarian Age:

> Astrology is an effective psycho-spiritual analytical tool . . . as the Aquarian Age unfolds, and man's understanding of himself and the cosmos becomes more manifest and creative, astrological truths will permeate the interrelated social order of the world. . . . Astrology is essentially religion. And the betrayer of religion is answerable to a power beyond this world.[18]

Astrology is intertwined in India's society. Some estimates indicate that ninety percent of the Indian population believes in astrology.[9] Even government officials look to astrological signs for guidance, and have tried to present astrology as a legitimate course in Indian universities.[10]

As I wandered through the crowded aisles, I came across the names of nearly every guru I had ever heard of. They were enthusiastically represented here by faithful devotees who sold their tapes and books and promoted their seminars. Their intensive courses were enormously expensive.

Pictures of "Jesus" were prominently displayed in some of the guru's booths. Many of them taught that Jesus studied under an Indian master before His baptism and subsequent ministry.

Of course this is impossible—the orthodox Jews would never have allowed Him to read Scripture in the synagogue if He had become "unclean" by studying among pagans. Worse yet, the gurus' other theories attempt to invalidate His death and resurrection. They claim that after facing death through meditation, Jesus eventually returned to India to gain further enlightenment. He was also said to be buried in Kashmir. Guru Sai Baba went so far as to make a film "proving" this Indian Jesus propaganda.

In other festive stalls, less pretentious than those of the gurus, a hodgepodge of other techniques and "opportunities" were promoted by zealous, friendly believers. Silva Mind Control (now called the Silva Method) promised that you could learn to use your mind to do anything you wished. Various martial arts experts offered Zen Buddhism's philosophy in an attractive package. Rolfing and rebirthing practitioners drew anxious seekers with promises of realigned energy and relived past lives.

The Music and the Mystical

All during this time, I tried to concentrate on the volumes of printed material I was being handed, but the strange sort of music I had first noticed on entering was robbing me of my concentration. What was it? It wasn't Indian, and yet it had a strange Eastern or Asian quality about it. Eventually, another brochure explained its sounds to me:

> New Age music, a unique style with no recognizable harmony, melody, or rhythm, is designed to relax listeners by aligning and attuning their bodies, minds, and spirits. Perfect for meditation, Yoga and massage, N.A. music is also gradually emerging as holistic background muzak in progressive restaurants, health centers, and dentists' offices around the country.

I spoke to one of the musicians there. He explained:

> For thousands of years, music has been used to induce altered states of consciousness. It's all tied together with Yoga and the chakras. Each chakra is associated with a color, an area of the body, and a tone. Each of these systems has seven members, seven colors, and seven chakras.

As he talked about the seven colors, I realized this was referring to rainbows. To me, the rainbow represented God's promise to man in Genesis 9:11-17. As I looked around this festival, I saw rainbows everywhere. I later discovered that in some New Age circles, the colors of the rainbow are called rays and are identified within the spectrum: red, orange, yellow, green, green-blue, blue, and purple. Correspondingly, each ray has a meaning, such as will, love, idealism, etc. It is believed that the final ray will eventually bring forth what occultist Alice Bailey called "the externalization of the hierarchy," at which point "the Christ" will "reappear."[11]

As I continued my excursion of the Mind, Spirit, Body festival, the music playing had a strong pull, appealing to all the senses. Pastor Larry DeBruyn, in his article, "The Music and the Mystical," says that some types of "music engenders mystical experiences." He explains:

> [T]here is much about music that is creative, experiential and ethereal. But as every genre from military marches to love songs indicates, some music possesses a mysterious, if not occult, power to sway the soul.[12]

Rob Bell, a contemporary pastor of *the emerging church* (a movement discussed in a later chapter), describes the role music played in his own spiritual journey:

> I remember the first time I was truly in awe of God . . . I was caught up for the first time in my life in something so massive and loving and transcendent and . . . true. Something I was sure could be trusted. I specifically remember thinking the universe was safe, in spite of all the horrible, tragic things in the world. I remember being overwhelmed by the word true. . . . I was sixteen and at a U2 concert. The Joshua Tree tour. When they started with the song "Where the Streets Have No Name," I thought I was going to spontaneously combust with joy. This was real. This mattered. Whatever it was, I wanted more. I had never felt that way before.[13]

Rob Bell's epiphany, which was birthed through a musical experience, has developed into a spirituality that Bell presents now to tens of thousands of people. Through his books, seminars, and Nooma films, he has become a major proponent for mystical spirituality. His book, *Velvet Elvis*, has sold over 250,000 copies and is used in Christian high schools, colleges, and universities. Pastor DeBruyn says that in many churches members are led "into dizzying realms of 'intimacy with God' through music." He adds:

> Misdirected spiritual hunger can produce a desire to throw off all restraint, and music can be the inducement. A quick glance at a rock concert crowd is very revealing. Hands in the air, bodies gyrating, and fans screaming in ecstasy are all the standard. Whipped into a frenzy by loud, pulsating music, they become unhinged, adopting a different model of behavior because of the atmosphere. . . .

> [T]he same basic mood pervades many congregations during worship time. Both the Brownsville Revival and the Toronto Blessing are noted for the unbiblical manifestations that often follow an extended song session.[14]

Perhaps one of the most unexpected displays I encountered that day so many years ago was seductively titled "The Mind Revolution: Four days that will change your life forever!" This seminar promised three steps to personal power. The first step was Energy, the second Skill, and the third Power. The new-found power was confirmed by an interesting new "Western" technique—firewalking. I hardly expected to encounter anything so blatantly Hindu in the Western world. But here it was!

Not far from the firewalking display was a booth for expectant mothers. In this setting were herbal remedies for common pregnancy maladies, books on prenatal Yoga, and an assortment of holistic birth materials. Bradley, Kitziner, and LaMaze techniques were all explained, each one advocating self-hypnosis: breathing, focusing, and centering.

The colors and sounds seemed to increase as I strolled through the rest of the exhibitions. At last I found my way to a quiet corner of the vast building. There I noticed that the political platform for the New Age was being subtly promoted. The intellectual-looking people manning the booths bore little resemblance to their wildly garbed psychic counterparts just across the hall. Nuclear freeze and disarmament were the concern of these Western pacifists with their Communist ties. This section of the fair seemed to have little to do with aura manipulation and tarot reading, but many gurus' booths were also advocating involvement in peace marches. Followers of Yogi Bhagan (of the 3HO Sikhs), Rajneesh, Buddhism, The Children of God, and Hare Krishna were all being encouraged to attend Stanford University's antinuclear conference, "The Meeting of the Ways."

I came upon a booth with a seminar focusing on "The Messiah and the Second Coming." It sounded so Christian, yet reading through its literature, I realized that another "christ" was being described and advocated. The material read:

> An in-depth evaluation and practical application of the levels of consciousness leading to the ultimate realization of Christ-consciousness, dealing with advanced techniques of meditation, inner purification of mind and emotion to the power of the word and the second birth.

Even the Christian "born-again-through-Christ" experience is now being counterfeited, I thought to myself. When I stop and ponder just how much the New Age has pervaded the 21st century Western culture, I find it nothing less than alarming. The new messiah promoted at the fair that day is identical to the "Coming One"[14] occultist Alice Bailey spoke of in a "prophecy" received from her spirit guide. Alarmingly, while many Christians claim they would never believe in such a false Christ because it would be just too obvious, the Christian church is being saturated with a mystical spirituality incorporating many Hindu and New Age practices and ideas.

Twelve

To Make Men Whole

I faced the long-awaited visit to my dentist with quiet resignation. *Another distraction from my work*, I sighed. As I settled back into the comfortable chair, I noticed a Christian fish plaque on the doctor's wall. Our conversation led from that to other related matters.

"So . . . what do you think of holistic medicine?" I asked, curious to hear his reply.

He chuckled. "That's an interesting question. In 1978, when I was attending a Christian university, we spelled *holism* with a *W*. In fact, our motto was 'To make man whole.' The medical school was as committed to healthy spiritual conditions as to healthy bodies."

"But here's the interesting part," he continued. "In 1979, a much-respected professor told us, 'We've got to rethink this *wholistic* concept. The rest of the medical community is dropping the *w* and confusing spiritual with mystical.'"

"This is interesting . . . so you feel that to a Christian wholism makes sense."

"Yeah. Sure. If the spirit is born again in Jesus, the mind and body have a far better chance of being healthy."

"But without Him," I added, "talk about spirituality is a different matter."

"Without Him, there is no spirituality."

Unfortunately, this dentist is in the minority when it comes to defining terms. Marilyn Ferguson's *The Aquarian Conspiracy* lists medicine as the most dynamic institution for transition into New Age thinking.[1]

What has happened to medicine? Thousands of M.D.s, Ph.D.s, chiropractors, and dentists are enthusiastic supporters of New Age holistic medicine. To quote from Marilyn Ferguson's book:

> For many Aquarian Conspirators, an involvement in health care was a major stimulus to transformation.
>
> A nurse said, "If healing becomes a reality with you, it's a lifestyle. Altered states of consciousness accompany it, increased telepathy. It's an adventure."
>
> Through that experience I became interested in learning more about hypnosis, biofeedback and meditation.[2]

Many hospitals have set up their own Yoga and meditation classes to provide stress reduction for patients, doctors, and nurses. Doctors and dentists who wouldn't think of promoting Christianity or Judaism on the grounds that they are religions are unwittingly involving their patients in Hindu practices.

Bookstores are inundated with health books that encourage the use of Yoga, meditation, Reiki, and other Eastern practices. *The Diabetic's Total Health Book* by June Biermann and Barbara Toohey devotes entire chapters to Yoga, biofeedback, meditation, and guided imagery. Several books addressing women's menopause are on the market, sold in major outlet bookstores: *A Meditation for Mastering Menopause* (CD), *Yoga and the Wisdom of Menopause*, and *Menopause with Science and Soul* are just a few. This latter book states: "Spiritual practice and meditation are keys to survival during menopause."[3] The book makes it clear that when it refers to meditation, it is talking about Eastern-style meditation. Instruction and information is offered on Yoga, mantras, chanting, and more.

One day I received a call from Sharon, a young Christian nurse. "Sorry to bother you," she began, "but I've run into a couple of things I don't understand."

"You sound worried."

"Well, I really am. At a hospital staff meeting, we were told that we could receive continuing education credits for attending the Mind Body Spirit Festival."

"Yes? Did you go?"

"Well, yeah. And I don't know what to think. Our seminar was on 'laying on of hands,' but the power we were supposed to be healing with wasn't the power of Jesus. At least they didn't call it that."

"What power do you think it was?"

"The facilitator said that we all have healing energy within us. Do we? Is it okay for me to think of it as being Jesus?"

Today, various types of *energy healing* pervade the medical/health field. The spirituality behind it is based on the Hindu chakra system, which includes use of psychic powers (through the third eye, opened at the sixth chakra) and ultimately embracing the divinity of man (at the seventh chakra). This is why chakra-based healing energy can never be divorced from the New Age movement; the two are inseparable. The numerous methods using healing energy go by a variety of names: Therapeutic Touch, Healing Touch, Reiki, Pranic Healing, Quantum Touch, and Deeksha (the Oneness Blessing).

The Oneness Blessing

While countless people in the Western world are now embracing mystical practices such as Yoga, Reiki, and contemplative meditation, most of them have probably not yet heard of the Oneness Movement.

The Oneness Movement is a fast growing effort to bring the *Oneness Blessing* to millions of people around the world with the hope of changing people's consciousness and thus the state of the planet. This Oneness experience takes place when a Oneness Blessing *giver* places his or her hands on a person's head (although it can also be bestowed through eye contact or even simple intention), and a sense of awakening into oneness is imparted.

According to an article in *Natural Awakenings* magazine, the Oneness Blessing is:

> Essentially a transfer of intelligent or divine energy from a Blessing giver to a Blessing receiver—the intention of which is meant to catalyze a realization of oneness with all forms of life on the planet, including the planet itself . . . and it is from this point that an evolutionary awakening in consciousness takes place.[4]

There are currently over 1300 trained Blessing givers in the US alone, and that number is growing steadily. There are 12,000 in India.[5] More and more people are accepting the Oneness Blessing, largely due to the growing acceptance of Yoga.

Behind the New Age consciousness transforming our society is a spiritual momentum, which seems to be increasing in scope and intensity. The Oneness Movement alone holds vast potential to greatly accelerate that transformation. It is estimated that tens of millions have already received the Oneness Blessing, and these are not just people in the New Age camp:

> [People] might be surprised to learn of numerous religious leaders—Christian, Catholic, and Muslim among others—who have embraced the Oneness Blessing and its vision of helping precipitate a global shift in consciousness.[6]

Currently, those interested in becoming Blessing givers must travel to India and take a twenty-one day course. If a similar center is established in the US or Canada (or both), then the number of participants can be expected to soar.

Tantra and "Spiritual Sex"?

Tantric sex incorporates mysticism into sexual activity. Couples, who seek out help for their relationships, are instructed to go into meditative states while being intimate. In her book, *Conjugal Spirituality* (which is promoted by Gary Thomas, a popular Christian author), Mary Anne McPherson Oliver discusses and encourages the use of tantric sex. Oliver suggests that "the Upanishads and Tantric writings [are] the basis of moral theology for couples" and that "mystical experiences can be associated with erotic love."[7] Oliver tells readers to use mantras and breath prayers to induce the tantric experience. She concludes with the following:

> Carl Jung predicted that the West would produce its own Yoga on the basis laid down by Christianity. I believe conjugal spirituality [tantra] to be just such a distinctively Western Yoga.[8]

In 1994 (when Oliver's book came out), she said the public wasn't quite ready for such a radical view of sexuality. But she spoke *optimistically* about the future because of the growing interest in mysticism in our society:

> Twentieth-century developments in mainstream theology have also prepared the way for the emergence of conjugal spirituality. An upsurge of interest in the spiritual life and a renaissance in mystical studies have widened the domain of spirituality.[9]

A July 2008 article in *The Vancouver Sun* gives a startling illustration of the validity of Oliver's statement. The Canadian newspaper article titled "Sex Brings Christians Closer to God" reports the growing acceptance of tantric sex. Chuck MacKnee, a professor at Trinity Western University (an evangelical school in British Columbia), has been researching and writing about "spiritual sex" (a Christian version of tantric sex), since the 1990s.[10]

MacKnee believes that "ultimately in sex we're going to meet God"; he says that "humans' relationship with God is essentially erotic." The *Sun* article observes that evangelicals who, like MacKnee, are "teaching about spiritual sex are in some ways catching up with Eastern-influenced New Age spirituality." It explains:

> Sensual spirituality has been popularized in the West through Hindu Tantric ritual, which links sexual energy with spiritual liberation.[11]

In a 1996 report titled "Peak Sexual and Spiritual Experience: Exploring the Mystical Relationship," MacKnee refers to mystics like John of the Cross and Teresa of Avila as examples of those who understood erotic spiritual experience. He says:

> It is significant to note that mystics have traditionally expressed their experience in the language of sexual love.[12]

He also says that sexuality involves entering "an altered state of consciousness."[13] Authors like MacKnee, Mary Anne McPherson Oliver, and Gary Thomas (who quotes Oliver twelve times in his popular Christian book *Sacred Marriage*) are closing the gap between Christianity and Eastern religion through their views on mystical sexuality.

As I have shown throughout this book, I believe that the spiritual realms entered during Eastern-style mediation, Yoga, tantra and so on are demonic realms. In view of this, the implications and probable effects of MacKnee and Oliver's work are disturbing.

An article titled "Can Sex Work be Shamanic?" illustrates the reason for my concern. It explains how its writer (a sex worker) became disillusioned with her line of work with men. After reading *Women of the Light: The New Sacred Prostitute,* she began integrating Buddhism, Chi Gung, Yoga, psychedelics and shamanism into her sessions. Now, giving herself to "multitudes of men" she says, "I have experienced myself becoming an embodiment of the goddess to the lives of those I touch."[14] What this woman does not understand is that this "embodiment" is the demonic realm of which I speak.

The Bible warns that the supernatural world can make contact with humans if a human gives permission for its entrance. That open door allows the spiritual being (sometimes seen as an angel of light: II Corinthians 11:14) to control whoever submits himself to its spiritual power (Genesis 6: 2 - 4).

Obviously these "heavenly" beings are not God's ministering angels who only do His bidding for His purposes, but they belong to Satan's legion, are possessed with his diabolical and rebellious source, and are known as fallen angels, a hierarchy of evil powers and principalities of wickedness (Ephesians 6:12).

Hypnotism

For centuries, certain Yogis have been able, with some regularity, to control bodily responses through the self-hypnotic discipline of Yoga. Are their techniques compatible with genuine Christian faith?

"What's the story?" A man cornered me at church one Sunday. "There's a fellow I know doing a hypnosis show over at the county fair. He claims to be a born-again Christian."

"Well, he may be. But he has a lot to learn about the occultic roots of his showbiz routine."

"He says there's nothing occultic about hypnosis. Anyone can do it. He says you just have to give in to the technique. Besides, it can't be dangerous because there are all kinds of tapes, records, and books on the subject. Even *Reader's Digest* says it works!"

While many people, even many Christians, think that hypnotism is a neutral technique, it actually relies on occultic (metaphysical) conditioning and has roots in reincarnation as research analyst and author Ray Yungen explains:

> Practically every practitioner of hypnosis I have come across during my years of research has had a noticeable bent toward metaphysics. Even if it seems unapparent at first, many hypnotherapists engage in such therapies

as past life regressions, which means that they accept reincarnation as being legitimate.[15]

Martin and Diedre Bobgan, in their well-respected 2001 study, *Hypnosis: Medical, Scientific, or Occultic,* state:

> We cannot call hypnosis a science, but we can say that it has been an integral part of the occult for thousands of years. E. Fuller Torrey, a research psychiatrist, aligns hypnotic techniques with witchcraft. He also says, "Hypnosis is one aspect of the Yoga techniques of therapeutic meditation" . . . If indeed hypnosis may result in occult healing, there are potential serious consequences to consider.[16]

The Bobgans, who have studied and written about hypnosis for years, conclude:

> Hypnotism is potentially dangerous at its best and is demonic at its worst. . . . Hypnosis is an altered state of consciousness, and there is no difference between the altered state of consciousness and the shamanic state of consciousness.[17]

One summer I had a once-in-a-lifetime opportunity to observe a group of hypnotized subjects being videotaped. These volunteers were performing various antics at the direction of their hypnotist. Some of their actions were hilarious, others obscene. One shy, soft-spoken woman in particular was unbelievably brazen and erotic in following the instructions she was given while in a trance.

Later the volunteers watched the videotape together. I interviewed the woman after she ran out of the room in tears, mortified by her behavior. She explained in embarrassment:

> I can't believe that was me up there . . . I'm telling you. I can't believe I would act like that. When I was hypnotized I do sort of remember what I was

doing, but I couldn't control what I did or what was happening. It was like watching somebody else. And even then I didn't know how gross I was acting. I had no idea . . . it just wasn't me. That's all I can say.

Her tear-streaked face and embarrassment told the tale. She had submitted her mind to someone else, and she was deeply regretful.

Submitting our minds to emptiness or another person's mind is unbiblical. Deuteronomy 18: 10-12 clearly instructs that the practice of casting charms or spells is an abomination to the Lord. This warning in itself should be sufficient to cause us to avoid this practice. We are to "gird up the loins" of our minds" (I Peter 1:13), "bringing into captivity every thought to the obedience of Christ" (II Corinthians 10:5), and to love the Lord with all our hearts, our souls, and our minds, as Jesus instructed (Matthew 22:37).

Guru Doctor of Medicine and Self-Help

D r. Dean Ornish is the founder and president of the Preventive Medicine Research Institute in Sausalito, California and also the Clinical Professor of Medicine at the University of California. In the 1970s, Ornish met Sri Swami Satchidananda (who was teaching Ornish's sister meditation techniques at the time) and told the guru he wanted to learn from him too. Today, he credits Satchidananda for inspiring his heart disease program. His book, *Program for Reversing Heart Disease*, became a *New York Times* best-seller and is a product of the swami's advice. Ornish says:

> Swami Satchidananda began teaching me in 1972 the meditation and Yoga techniques that evolved into the stress management program described [in this book]. Since then, he has remained my teacher and close friend.[18]

Ornish devotes two chapters in his book to Yoga and other meditative techniques, explaining that "Yoga is a system of powerful tools for achieving union . . . with a higher force,"[19] and through meditation, the higher self can be experienced. Quoting Swami Vivekananda, he states:

> In one word, this ideal is that you are divine . . . All
> the powers in the universe are already ours.[20]

Ornish was appointed to the White House Commission on Complementary and Alternative Medicine Policy by former President Clinton and also served as a physician consultant to Clinton and several bipartisan members of the U.S. Congress. His influence in the field of alternative medicine has had far reaching effects upon the medical profession as a whole.

Any doubts you may have that New Age concepts have saturated both the medical and psychological aspects of the modern-day health field can easily be dispelled. You need only visit your local bookstore and check the medical and self-help sections. You will find the majority of books take a stance derived from Hindu (Eastern) philosophy that proclaims the divinity of man realized through meditative exercises. Even Christian bookstore shelves display books that promote Eastern-style meditation and other unbiblical practices.

As life becomes increasingly stressful, more and more people will buy into the lie that mysticism—and finding the divinity within—is the key to living a whole and healthy life. But this is not true. Scripture tells us that the answer lies not in our own power, but in God's, through Jesus Christ alone.

By His power, and perhaps with the help of a biblically sound friend or advisor, we can deal with any person. We can solve any problem. We can face any foe. We can be healed of any emotional wounds.

> According as his divine power hath given unto
> us all things that pertain unto life and godliness,
> through the knowledge of him that hath called us
> to glory and virtue. (II Peter 1:3)

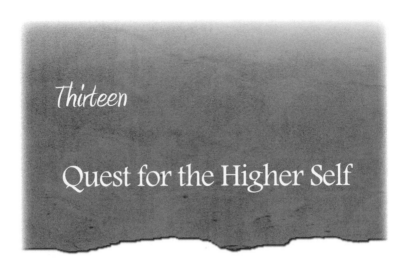

Thirteen

Quest for the Higher Self

C heryl sat in my office and tearfully told me her strange story. Just the day before, her pastor had taken her by the hands as he counseled her. The dimly lit room had been hushed. He unfolded her tightly-closed fists and gently pressed her palms against his desk. Then he barely touched his own fingertips against hers.

"Now close your eyes," he quietly instructed. "Picture yourself as a tiny child. Do you remember being two years old?"

"Yes". . . Cheryl's voice broke.

"That's right. You're hurt and confused. Your father has just left you alone after an abusive incident." Cheryl began to sob.

"You're all by yourself. Frightened. You're wearing only your diapers and a little shirt. There is a knock on the door. You go to the door and open it. Suddenly the room is flooded with dazzling light. It's Jesus!"

"Jesus . . ." Cheryl whispered in a childlike voice.

"Yes, Jesus. Now tell Him what's happened. Ask Him what to do. Let Him counsel you."

At this point the pastor-counselor quietly left the room. Cheryl was sobbing convulsively, and he had instructed her to have her own "private" conversation with this Jesus.

Cheryl had come to me because the experience had somehow seemed mystical or "magical." It had frightened her spiritually and she didn't know why. To me, such conjuring was alarmingly reminiscent of Hindu spiritual experiments and experiences. I remembered conversations with occultic gurus who openly encouraged and taught these techniques. Spirit guides are visualized and confronted. Such Hindu techniques have been cultivated for centuries.

Now, however, on a daily basis in dozens of Christian counseling sessions, the same practices are being used. Jesus is visualized, animated in the mind of the patient, and sought for counsel. When this visualized Jesus speaks, his words are accepted as the very words of God.

Counselors who take part in this sort of visualization therapy (often called *inner healing*—a term popularized by Ruth Carter Stapleton) explain that Jesus is "the same yesterday, today, and forever." They believe that the patient either didn't know Him or didn't turn to Him at the time of some particular crisis, so the circumstances simply need to be reenacted with Him present.

To a person such as myself, who has been exposed to the Hindu concept of *maya* (that life is an illusion), this method becomes particularly suspect. Can we mentally create an "envisioned Jesus" to speak to us at our whim? What makes us think we can manipulate the God of the universe to appear at our every request? How can we be sure we've contacted the real Jesus?

When Jesus actually did appear following His resurrection it was always in His own time and on His own terms. He came to encourage—to reinforce faith. Never is there a report in Scripture of His being mentally pictured, soon materializing with sage advice.

The two disciples on the Emmaus Road had known Jesus personally. They were lost in grief, on their way home following the nightmarish events of the crucifixion. Joined by an unidentified stranger, they didn't know Him to be Jesus until after He had blessed and broken bread with them and vanished. Speaking of the time while they were on the road with Him, they said, "Did not our heart burn within us?" (Luke 24:32). Their spirits had recognized Him, but not their eyes!

John's encounter with Christ after His ascension (in his Patmos vision) caused him to fall on his face in awe. John had shared a very special relationship with Jesus. John was the one "whom Jesus loved" (John 13:23), who lay against His bosom at the Last Supper. John had seen Him transfigured, had watched Him die, and had met Him after His resurrection. Yet the awesome, glorified Jesus was almost unrecognizable as the human John had known.

Decades before John's encounter with the ascended, glorified Christ on Patmos, however, in another appearance to His disciples after His crucifixion, Jesus addressed Thomas. What He said at that time is extremely important for us in these days of deception. Thomas, after expressing grave doubts about Jesus' resurrection, met his living Lord face to face. Jesus knew Thomas had been unconvinced of His resurrection and invited him to touch the scars of His wounds. The relieved disciple proclaimed, "My Lord and my God" (John 20:28).

Jesus' response to Thomas' declaration has echoed down through twenty centuries to the sanctuaries of our experience-hungry churches:

> [B]ecause thou hast seen me, thou hast believed: blessed are they that have not seen, and yet have believed. (John 20:29)

Creative Visualization

The current popularity of visualization techniques is largely due to a woman named Shakti Gawain. Her book, *Creative Visualization,* teaches that we can, in essence, create our own reality. Her teaching goes beyond the boundaries of a normal use of the imagination—it delves into the supernatural, mystical world where one can conjure up beings from the spirit realm and alter the course of the future. Gawain considers these *spirit guides* friends who can help us through life: "Many people who have established a relationship with their guide meet them every day in their meditation."[1] But as do all New Age thinkers, Gawain believes that man shares divinity with God. "There is no separation between us and God,"[2] she states. She calls this "our divine potential."[3]

How do visualization techniques line up with the Christian faith? The Bible says that the "blessed hope" of the church is the physical return of Jesus Christ to earth (Titus 2:13). But if we are longing for a mystical experience that will somehow bring Him into view now, we need to weigh our desires against biblical principles. God is not a shimmering puppet whom we can control with our own cleverly devised mental strings: He is a Spirit, a person separate from ourselves, and we must worship Him in spirit and in truth.

We must test all spirits, as the apostle John instructed. To the New Ager, God appears as light. The Bible warns that Satan comes as an angel of light (II Corinthians 11:14), but that Jesus is the *real* Light of the world. So what can we do to be sure that our "visions" and our "messages" are from the true God? "[E]very spirit that confesseth not that Jesus Christ is come in the flesh is not of God" (I John 4:3). Jesus is God's only-begotten Son. He died on the Cross for our sins. He was raised from the dead on the third day. He is fully God and fully human. He *is* the Christ, not a bearer of the *christ-consciousness*.

Unfortunately, many Christians don't understand that there are other spiritual sources of power besides Jesus. For every true gift, there is a counterfeit, and many people are using the counterfeit power, often through visualization. This reminds me very much of my own former use of psychic powers. In fact, visualization or *imaging* is unrelated to anything I have ever learned from the Bible. Norman Vincent Peale described the technique in his book *Positive Imaging*:

> As the years went by, I began using imaging techniques whenever I wanted to achieve a certain goal. In my second little church, located in Brooklyn, New York, attendance was low; in fact one day I

found the sexton dragging one of the back pews out of the building. When I asked him why, he said he was going to chop it up for firewood. "No one sits in it anyway," he explained.

"Put it back," I told him grimly. "Somebody is going to sit in it!" I visualized that pew full, and all the other pews full, and the church filled to capacity. I held that image in my mind. I worked for it with every ounce of strength I had. I made it part of my innovative thinking. And the day came when the image became a reality. . . .

Perhaps the idea of the power of positive thinking was conveyed to me right then and there. But behind that idea, and in it, and beyond it was the concept of imaging—holding the *image* of yourself succeeding, visualizing it so vividly that when the desired success comes, it seems to be merely echoing a reality that has already existed in your mind.[4]

Norman Vincent Peale's positive thinking is nothing short of faith in faith. This has been substituted for faith in our God. And faith in our faith is nothing short of faith in ourselves: our wills, our desires, our minds, even our subconscious minds and illusions—in other words, our dreams.

The Secret and The Moses Code

In 2006, a book (and a DVD with the same name) called *The Secret* by Rhonda Byrne was released and made extremely popular through Oprah Winfrey's promotion. *The Secret*'s objective is to let the world know that humanity is on the brink of a new era. This new era will open up humanity to unlimited power, riches, creativity and all that we ever dreamed of. A "secret" that has been locked away for centuries is now available to all. One news source explains just how *The Secret* works:

In the film [DVD], viewers learn to ask for what they want. And, if they believe it, they will receive it.

It sounds simple enough, but here's the catch: If you're cynical, sad, depressed and resigned that nothing will change, nothing will. Thoughts are so powerful, the teachers insist, that you attract what you think about, even if you don't want it. Get it?[5]

The Secret uses teachers from the past and present to reveal a hidden knowledge. Present day teachers include Jack Canfield (Chicken Soup for the Soul), John Gray (Men Are From Mars, Women Are From Venus), and an assortment of philosophers, writers, and visionaries who share their insights on the "secret." One of The Secret teachers explains:

We have a magnificent inner calling, vision, mission, power inside us that we are not honoring and harnessing . . . This movie brings it to the forefront that we can [harness that power].[6]

Larry King calls The Secret the "most profound information [he] has run across in forty years."[7]

The Secret focuses on the Law of Attraction; Australian-born creator of the project, Rhonda Byrne, who after a series of setbacks in her own life, said she discovered that past personalities like Albert Einstein, Thomas Edison, William Shakespeare, and Abraham Lincoln had a secret knowledge. Byrne came to believe this secret "was part of every religion, including Christianity, Hinduism and Buddhism."[8]

The DVD trailer begins by showing a genie from a lamp, who tells the lamp holder "your wish is my command."[9] The following explanation of this genie concept helps us to understand its significance:

[The] genie represent[s] the higher self, who was reached through meditation by staring at the flame of an oil lamp. It was believed that a person could have whatever he or she wanted, once in touch with it. Our word *genius* comes from this Latin word for spirit guide and now means a person with great creative power.[10]

The premise of *The Secret* is that we all have a divine essence within us, and we just need to get in touch with it. In other words, as panentheists teach, God is in all of creation, including all human beings, and once a person becomes aware of this, there are no limits to what he can achieve:

> Once a person merges with the higher self, he is on his way to empowerment, meaning he is capable of creating his own reality. Basically, all power is within the higher self, so when one is in tune with it, he can run his own show. . . .
>
> Metaphysicians believe that we all create our own circumstances anyway, so when we are guided and empowered by our higher self, we can consciously *co-create* with it.[11]

What most people who read the book or view the DVD do not know is that Rhonda Byrne is a disciple of a couple named Jerry and Esther Hicks. In the acknowledgements section of *The Secret* book, Byrne thanks the Hicks and "the teachings of Abraham." Abraham is a group of spirit guides that Esther Hicks channels for guidance on spiritual issues. On the Hicks' website, it states:

> Abraham, a group of obviously evolved teachers, speak their broader Non-Physical perspective through the physical body of Esther [Hicks]. Speaking to our level of comprehension . . . through a series of loving, allowing, brilliant yet comprehensively simple, recordings in print, in video, and in sound—they guide us to a clear

connection with our Inner Being—they guide us
to self-upliftment from our total self [god-self].[12]

Over two years after its release, *The Secret* remains on the *New
York Times* Best Seller List. A sequel to *The Secret*, *The Moses Code*,
came out in the Spring of 2008, also in both book and DVD format.
Quoting many of the same people as its predecessor, *The Moses Code*
took the concepts presented in *The Secret* a giant step further. The
publisher of *The Moses Code* reveals the theme of the project:

> Is it possible that nearly 3,500 years ago, Moses was
> given the secret for attracting everything you've ever
> desired? The Moses Code was first used to create
> some of the greatest miracles in the history of the
> world, but then it was hidden away, and only the
> highest initiates were allowed to practice it. . . . By
> practicing the principles presented within these
> pages, you'll discover how you can integrate the
> most powerful manifestation tool in the history of
> the world into your own life.[13]

The Moses Code, like *The Secret*, teaches the Law of Attraction, which, if practiced faithfully, promises to help one obtain
his or her hopes and dreams. But unlike *The Secret*, which focuses
primarily on personal goals and desires, *The Moses Code* takes
followers down a different direction:

> You may have been told that this Law is all about
> "getting" the things you want—things that you think
> will make your life more satisfying. But what if that's
> just the first step, and cracking the Moses Code depends
> more on what you're willing to "give" rather than "get."
> That would mean that you have the power to create
> miracles in your life right now! . . . You're here to use
> the power of Divinity itself to create a world based on
> the laws of compassion and peace.[14]

The emphasis of *The Moses Code* is the term "I AM." I AM (translated as "Jehovah" or "Yahweh" in English Bibles) is the name in Hebrew by which God identified Himself to Moses and the nation of Israel (Exodus 3:13-15). In a promotional trailer preview of *The Moses Code* DVD, viewers are instructed to repeat "I AM" statements to themselves to help affirm their own divinity and power.[15] In one segment of the trailer, a man applies to himself the claim of Jesus Christ recorded in John 14:6, by stating, "I am the way, I am the truth, I am the light [life]." In other words, viewers should call themselves God!

The Moses Code says that mysticism is the method through which we can enter "frequencies" that draw us into a sacred space called the "Divine Energy." These frequencies can be entered by turning to the "I AM THAT I AM field"[16] which:

> help[s] initiate and enhance sacred experiences. . . . the potential is promising, particularly with regard to assisting the I AM THAT I AM breathing exercises . . . developed for *The Moses Code*.[17]

While *The Secret* focuses on the law of attraction (which it claims is made possible because *all is One*), *The Moses Code* much more blatantly claims we are all divine by encouraging the reader or viewer to refer to himself as the "I AM" of the Bible.

Nowhere in the Bible does it indicate that we are to take on such a view in order to find out the secrets of God. The prophet Daniel said "there is a God in heaven that revealeth secrets." But Jesus told His disciples that these secrets or mysteries would be revealed only to those who believe on Him:

> Unto you it is given to know the mysteries of the kingdom of God: but to others in parables; that seeing they might not see, and hearing they might not understand. (Luke 8:10)

Contemplative Spirituality

Our world is quickly becoming a mystical world. This may be difficult for many to believe because the meaning of mysticism is not commonly understood. Many people don't even believe mysticism is real, saying things like, "The New Age is nothing but silliness," or "That is just a lot of nonsense." But the supernatural world and contacting it through mystical practices is anything but silly. It is serious and dangerous business! Throughout the Bible it states that a spiritual realm exists, one that cannot be seen with human eyes. Scripture also says there are spiritual beings called angels; some are holy, some are fallen. Satan is a very real, malignant, powerful, and clever spiritual being.

Unfortunately, many Christians are experimenting with mysticism through what New Age author of *The Aquarian Conspiracy*, Marilyn Ferguson, calls "Christian mysticism."[18] This so-called Christian mysticism leads people into New Age thinking through an experience often referred to as *cosmic consciousness, unity consciousness*, or *god-consciousness*. This is the same *all-is-one* experience that I first ran into while using drugs and then later while practicing Yoga.

Having practiced Eastern meditation through Yoga, I honestly believe *Christian* (i.e., *contemplative*) mediation is a treacherous counterfeit and an absolute deception. Christians are being led to practice Eastern-style meditation through *contemplative prayer*, *centering prayer* or *entering the silence*. These practices can lead a Christian to contact a spirit guide disguised as one of God's angels, or as Jesus Himself.[19]

One of the foremost teachers of *contemplative spirituality* is Richard Foster, a Quaker speaker and writer who emulates the beliefs of Catholic mystics like Thomas Merton, Thomas Keating, and Basil Pennington (the forerunners of the modern-day contemplative prayer movement). In his best-selling book, *Celebration of Discipline*, Foster tells readers to "enroll" in the practice of contemplative prayer,[20] saying we "should stop to reflect and to treasure the words, to turn them over and over in our minds, repeating them."[21] To understand more fully Foster's view of contemplative prayer, read what he says about a Benedictine monk named John Main:

> Dom John Main understood well *the value* of both silence and solitude. . . . Main rediscovered meditation while living in the Far East.[22]
>
> (emphasis added)

Main "rediscovered meditation" from his Hindu guru, Swami Satyananda from whom he "recognized the practice of the mantra"[23] and came to use it in prayer sessions three times a day.[24] Main died in 1982, but he left a "legacy" known as *the way of the mantra*, and many have been influenced by his beliefs. Richard Foster is one of those, and he has carried on with the contemplative message to millions of Christians.

Since the release of *Celebration of Discipline* in 1978, contemplative spirituality has entered countless mainstream and evangelical churches and organizations. While Foster and Main understood the Eastern roots of this kind of prayer, most Christians practicing contemplative do not realize they are engaging in the very meditative practices that gurus in India have practiced for centuries.

The reason for this is that Merton, Keating, and Pennington credit the modern day mystical movement to the Desert Fathers, monks who lived during the second and third centuries and engaged in mystical practices including times of deep silent meditation.

Many have speculated as to how the Desert Fathers came to learn this way of meditation. Daniel Goleman, New Age author of *The Meditative Mind*, gives this valid explanation:

> The meditation practices and rules for living of these earliest Christian monks bear strong similarity to those of their Hindu and Buddhist renunciate brethren several kingdoms to the east. While Jesus and his teachings were their inspiration, the meditative techniques they adopted for finding their God suggest either a borrowing from the East or a spontaneous rediscovery.[24\]

What is not understood by contemplatives is that: 1. Christian contemplative prayers and meditation are identical with Eastern mantras and Eastern meditation; 2. When Eastern meditation is practiced, and "silence" is achieved, it produces an altered state of mind; 3. Eastern meditative techniques, even if applied as "Christian" and called "contemplative prayer" etc., begin to change the meditators spiritual outlook. The practitioner's altered state justifies any anti-biblical reasoning. The use of the technique gives way to delusion and deception (Romans 1:28) because the heart is desperately wicked (Jeremiah 17:9) and out of it comes evil thought (Matthew 15:19).

Because demonic realms are entered during the contemplative silence, over time meditators lose their confidence in God's Word, which states that Jesus Christ is God, and because of His death and resurrection, the only way to salvation. Thus, this form of meditation has become one of Satan's greatest tools of deception, leading people away from Christ and toward a lie. In view of all this, what should we be doing? The Bible gives us sound and sure instruction:

> Study to shew thyself approved unto God, a workman
> that needeth not to be ashamed, rightly dividing the
> word of truth. (II Timothy 2:15)

> Thy word have I hid in mine heart, that I might not
> sin against thee. (Psalm 119:11)

> Wherefore take unto you the whole armour of God,
> that ye may be able to withstand in the evil day, and
> having done all, to stand. (Ephesians 6:13)

And let us "earnestly contend for the faith which was once delivered unto the saints" (Jude 3).

Satan is the mastermind behind New Age thinking, and his plan is to "deceiveth the whole world" (Revelation 12:9). He wants to change the minds of billions, to restructure, recondition, and reprogram them as rapidly as possible. And he is doing it successfully, unbeknownst to the masses.

Fourteen

Yoga Uncoiled

I n 2006, I returned again to India, this time with a production crew to work on the film, *Yoga Uncoiled*.* We interviewed both Christians and Hindus to get their perspectives on Yoga, Hinduism, and Yoga's major influx into our Western society. Our findings were quite astounding.

Yoga's Surprising Popularity

T oday, somewhere between fifteen and twenty million North Americans practice Yoga, with over 70,000 Yoga teachers.[1] Yoga is offered in eighty percent of health clubs, promoted on TV as body toning and flexibility exercises, and offered to corporate employees as a medical benefit to steady the mind, calm the emotions and relax away stresses. A 2008 study released by *Yoga Journal* on "Yoga in America" revealed that eighteen million Americans are interested in practicing Yoga, and Americans are currently spending 5.7 billion dollars a year on Yoga classes and related

---

* This chapter is adapted from the film *Yoga Uncoiled*.

products, including mats, books, DVDs, and clothing.[2] Nearly half of current practitioners started doing Yoga "to improve their overall health."[3] Bill Harper, publisher of *Yoga Journal* stated that "Yoga is no longer simply a singular pursuit but a lifestyle choice and an established part of our health and cultural landscape."[4]

Until the late 1990s, the Christian church recognized Yoga as part of the Hindu religion. Now, however, Yoga is actually being practiced by Christians. It is promoted as Christian *mind-body fitness* and as a spiritual vehicle to enhance the Christian walk.

How did India's Eastern mysticism gain access into the West in so short a time? How did Hinduism change its message to make it acceptable to the West? For answers, we need only go back to the 1960s, to the birth of the hippie generation, the psychedelic drug culture, and the heroes of that era—The Beatles.

How the East Came to the West

In 1967, the Beatles journeyed to Rishnekesh, India, home of Maharishi Mahesh Yogi, founder of Transcendental Meditation. Their endorsement of Transcendental Meditation, which soon became known as TM, introduced millions of their fans to Hinduism's Yoga.

The lure of Eastern mysticism continued to grow as the hippie generation began to realize the similarities between the altered states attained by the practice of Yoga and those attained by drug use. Hinduism became quite appealing and readily accepted by many because it not only permits drug use for religious trances, but it enables its followers to shift states of consciousness without necessarily using drugs.

George Harrison became a dedicated member of Hinduism's Hari Krishna consciousness movement, established by Swami Prabhupada In his lackluster hit song, *My Sweet Lord*, Harrison effectively blended Eastern religion with traditional Western thought. He became the first to successfully inject New Age mysticism into contemporary popular music. He created *spiritual fusion* by interchanging the names of Eastern deities like Krishna and Rama with the biblical worship terms of *hallelujah* and *Lord God*.

The Beatles' syncretism began the cultural revolution. Indian mystics, gurus, swamis, yogis, and bagwans invaded the West, becoming familiar household names, as did the names of various types of Eastern meditation, including Yoga.

Even religious Hindu disciplines like vegetarianism and teachings such as reincarnation became positive spiritual options to Western thinking.

Two other factors came into play to enable India's Eastern mysticism to infiltrate the Western culture within so short a time: Yoga's secularization and the increasing stresses of modern life.

Yoga's Hindu spiritual aspects were down-played, and it was repackaged as a system of exercises and meditation that focused on releasing the body's energy stored in the spine and calming the mind.

At the same time, the Western lifestyle became increasingly stressful. Where there is stress, there are health problems. Alleviating stress is the number one reason that people seek out the altered state of consciousness that Yoga imparts.

The Beatles perform at the Cow Palace in San Francisco. Paul McCartney, John Lennon and George Harrison on stage—1965

"Christian Yoga"

Many people try to separate the exercises of Yoga from its spiritual element. The secular, intellectual West has long assumed it can divorce yogic practice from its spiritual aspects simply by ignoring or redefining them.

Similarly, the Western church has come to assume it may safely Christianize Yoga, which it once viewed as a heathen import from the East and taboo for Christians. Yoga is now accepted as benign, and a wave of spiritually-based aerobic workout alternatives packaged in Christian terminology has washed over the Western world. These combine Yoga movements, postures, breathing concentration, and repetitive prayer with Christian themes, music, prayers, and worship, or biblical verses and names.

What's more, Eastern meditation in general has been given a new "look." For example, Thomas Keating, in his book, *Open Mind, Open Heart*, renames Eastern meditation techniques as "centering," "contemplative prayer," and "transformed into Christ."[5] To add to this fusion between the East and the West, leading Christian publishers are releasing numerous books and videos on Yoga for Christians.

As a result of this changing attitude toward Yoga and Eastern mysticism, a growing number of Christian churches are offering programs for both the community and their own members that "blend" Christianity and mystical practices such as Yoga.

Time magazine featured an article titled "Stretching for Jesus," which reported on the controversy over "Christian Yoga." It featured Cindy Senarighi, a Lutheran pastor and the founder of "Yoga Devotion." Senarighi teaches Yoga in her Lutheran church in Minnesota. According to *Time*, such classes are part of a "fast-growing movement that seeks to retool the 5,000-year-old practice of Yoga to fit Christ's teachings."[6]

Although Senarighi receives opposition to her teaching from both fundamental Hindus and fundamental Christians, she says there is "a huge, wide group of people right down the middle who understand Yoga in a different way than either of those groups do."[7] She explains:

> They understand the Western practice of Yoga, the physical use, the physical practice of Yoga, being not only good for them physically, but emotionally, and as I said, spiritually—being able to be in prayer and meditation.[8]

Senarighi believes that if Christian words are used as the mantras (which Yoga meditation requires), or the intent in using Yoga is to reach Jesus, then it is perfectly all right to combine Yoga and Christianity. She says:

> One of the ways that I encourage my students to bring their Yoga practice and a Christian spiritual practice together, is to think about a favorite Bible verse or Scripture, or any Christian mantra such as the word "Jesus" or "amen," and connect that with their body and their mind and their spirit in practice.[9]

North American women in a Yoga class

Another Yoga teacher mentioned in the *Time* magazine article is Susan Bordenkircher, a Methodist from Alabama and the author of *Yoga for Christians*, a book published by Thomas Nelson (one of the largest Christian publishers). Bordenkircher discovered Yoga in 2002:

> "I knew right away I was getting something out of it spiritually and physically, but it felt uncomfortable in that format," she says. So Bordenkircher prepared a vinyasa, or series of postures, with a biblical bent. Meditations focus on Jesus. She calls the sun salutation, a series of poses honoring the Hindu sun god, a "warm-up flow" instead.[10]

The *Time* article reveals that "Yoga purists" (Hindus) are bothered by the idea of "Christian Yoga," saying that "Hinduism is not like a recipe ingredient that can be extracted from Yoga."[11] At the Hindu University of America in Orlando, Florida, a professor of Yoga philosophy and meditation states, "Yoga is Hinduism."[12]

Yoga has entered the Christian church through the notion that it is all right to adapt the Hindu practice of Yoga by using Christian terms and concepts; as long as only the exercises are practiced without meditation, Yoga is safe. Neither notion could be further from the truth. Former Hindu guru Rabi Maharaj, in his autobiography *Death of a Guru*, states, "No part of Yoga can be separated from the philosophy behind it."[13] Hinduism is totally incompatible with genuine, biblical Christianity—the two cannot be absorbed into one. There simply cannot be any such thing as "Christian Yoga." Let's look at why separating Hindu spirituality from Yoga exercises is not possible.

What's It All About, Yogi?

To understand what Yoga is really all about, one must understand that its origins are purely religious; classical Hinduism and Yoga are synonymous.

Hinduism Today, a leading Indian publication, admits that "Hinduism is the soul of Yoga," since Yoga is based on Hindu scripture and was developed by Hindu sages.[14]

Yoga's religious purpose is two-fold: to gain control over the body and to open the mind into altered states of consciousness. To understand the need for the latter, one must understand and believe in the Hindu way of looking at God.

Hinduism asserts that the universe we live in and are part of is a manifestation of the supreme being Brahma, the infinite, all-embracing, ever blissful consciousness.

Hinduism regards everything as part of the deity—the cows on the street, the monkeys in the city, the idols of half man-, half animal-like creatures. But Hinduism's highest goal is to enable individuals to come to god-consciousness: the realization of their personal divinity. Hindu priests developed rituals they called *Yoga* specifically to enable their followers to arrive at this realization.

The Bhagavad Gita, a sacred Hindu text, teaches that supreme joy comes to whoever practices Yoga, because he becomes one with the Hindu god Brahman, the cosmic consciousness.

According to Harish Johari, Indian scholar and tantra practitioner, *Yoga* means "union," referring to the union of the individual's consciousness with the cosmic consciousness and is based on "disciplines and exercises" that unite "individual and cosmic consciousness."[15] Johari says "[t]here are many different yoga traditions and practices, which in essence have the same goal: the union with the divine."[16]

Through Hatha Yoga's physical exercises, one gains control over the body, enabling one to meditate more intensely, and to open pathways in the spine for the flow of Kundalini energy.

Yoga uses a set of techniques to raise the coiled Kundalini energy through the seven chakras. The realization of being one with the universe, and thus, of being divine, comes as the result of the Kundalini serpent power, recognized as psychic energy, traveling up the spine through the chakras:

> Chakras represent specific psychophyscial energies
> that are activated one by one through the breath. . . .
> Aroused by the practices of tantra yoga, the dormant
> spiritual Kundalini energy can be made to leave the
> first chakra and pierce the chakras above causing
> various spiritual experiences to occur.[17]

The first five chakras are said to be located along the spine, from its base to the throat.

Hindus believe god-consciousness is attained deep within the part of the mind known as *the seat of concentrated wisdom*. It is situated in the sixth chakra, between the eyebrows. The sixth chakra is the first chakra of higher consciousness. Self-realization is supposed to occur when the Kundalini power flowing into it opens the third eye. The third eye is a central point, where all experience is gathered in total concentration. The seventh chakra is located at the top of the skull.

Hatha Yoga, in raising the coiled Kundalini energy from the base of the spine through the seven chakras, brings about the union of Hinduism's divine mother Shakti, in the form of the serpentine Kundalini force, with the god Shiva, the destroyer of ignorance, believed to reside in "eternal bliss" in the seventh chakra at the top of the skull.[18] When the Kundalini energy is released, body movements become serpent-like.

It is important to understand that the results of Yoga are real: the exercises and breathing techniques actually do release an energy and bring a change in consciousness. Our secular society ignores the remarkable similarities between drug abuse and mystical practices. The goal of both drug abuse and Yoga meditation is to shut down from life's reality. Both produce physiological changes in the body and brain and (some very dangerous) euphoric experiences. Drug use is illegal and the public is alerted of its dangers. Yoga, however, is endorsed as a beneficial mind-body exercise.

Yoga . . . By Any Other Name

Just because Yoga is used by Christians does not change the origin or nature of the energy or altered state of consciousness it brings. Whether called Kundalini or *the spine's untapped energy* or some Christian name, the same energy is released. "Christian Yoga" exercise and meditation brings about exactly the same state of altered consciousness as Hatha Yoga, New Age meditation, and hallucinogenic drugs. So, what is the source?

> [Eastern] meditation is to detach [your mind] because Eastern meditation teaches us that a rational mind cannot find or cannot reach the absolute truth. So you have to cut off all your rational thinking and emotions so that your mind will be empty so that you can reach the realization [of being] one with the universe.[19]

To experience the stilling or emptying of the mind, Yoga practitioners must first master the physical postures and movements of Yoga meditation. The physical exercises, themselves a religious Hindu ritual, are designed to bring a person into contact with spiritual beings. Speaking of her Yoga sessions, Cindy Senarighi said she noticed she was "in the presence of God in a way that I had never been before. The more I practiced, the more I experienced God's presence."[20]

Yoga positions facilitate altered states of mind so that one may experience a mystical presence. But does Yoga facilitate God's presence? Can the use of a mantra or Yoga meditation really bring Christ into our lives? George Alexander, author of *Yoga, the Truth Behind the Posture*, answers this important question:

> You cannot force Jesus to come into your life. But [a] mantra is something that . . . force[s] a spirit to come into your life. [The] Bible very clearly teaches you cannot force the Spirit of God to come into your life by repeating His name.[21]

The Bible teaches that the presence of God cannot be manipulated by man's desire for His presence. One is granted access to the biblical God only through Jesus Christ His Son, who declared, "I am the way, the truth, and the life: no man cometh unto the Father, but by me" (John 14:6).

The born-again Christian has a personal connection with God because of the saving grace of Jesus Christ. Jesus has promised to abide with us as we abide in Him through His grace and the power of His Spirit. There are no body movements or special positions necessary to bring one into communion with God's Spirit. The only connection to God has been made by Jesus Christ Himself.

Demons, however, easily make contact with individuals using visualization, imaging techniques, mantras, and so forth. They are able to manipulate people's minds, to make themselves appear as benevolent or superior beings or even as Jesus Christ Himself. Through Eastern meditation techniques, many mistake evil spirits appearing as Jesus for the actual Jesus Christ. The real Jesus is the only way to God the Father—no one else can also be a way to God—not Mary, not an angel, not a spirit claiming to be Jesus, not any other being.

God is not deceived by appearances. Putting Christian labels on conjuring techniques does not change His mind about them. Whatever conjures up a spirit is always an offense to Him and sin for us. Whether ignorantly conjuring up a spirit by the Kundalini energy released by Yoga exercises, or deliberately conjuring up spirit guides through meditation, the silence, contemplative prayer, it is all part of enchantment or divination: "discovering things secret by the aid of superior beings, or other than human means."[22] God clearly forbids this kind of activity:

> Ye shall not eat any thing with the blood: neither shall ye use enchantment, nor observe times. . . . Regard not them that have familiar spirits, neither seek after wizards, to be defiled by them: I am the LORD your God. (Leviticus 19:26, 31)

Interestingly, George Alexander says that the serpent "is a very prominent deity" in Hinduism. He explains the significance:

> If you look in the picture of Lord Shiva in Hinduism, you see a snake wrapped around his neck. They believe that the serpent power is in every person and the serpent power is sleeping in you. By practicing Yoga, it awakens that Kundalini power in you. . . . [W]hen the Kundalini power is awakened, that goes up to the brain and awakens the psychic power.[23]

This is why the positions in Yoga are so important; they are based on serpents' movements to facilitate the flow of the Kundalini serpent energy. Western Yoga practitioners think this energy is a neutral force. It is not. Yoga exercises do not release the energy from within a person's own spine. The sensations of Kundalini energy and an altered state of consciousness are produced by a demonic presence.

Most cultures view the serpent positively and worship it for its wisdom. Only the Bible describes the serpent as man's enemy, a usurper who wishes to take the Creator God's rightful place in the mind of mankind. In Hinduism, the serpent (Kundalini) is believed to be awakened through Yoga meditation, granting the practitioner an awareness of *God*, a stillness, a god-consciousness.

The Bible records that Satan, in the serpent, cunningly beguiled Eve and seduced her mind, corrupting her from a sincere, whole-hearted and pure devotion to God. He deceived her into believing a lie: that she, through her mind, could be like God. Ironically, Yoga, through arousal of snake power, the mind-altering experience of the Kundalini spirit in the body, continues to deceive all its practitioners with the same lie.

How Hinduism Changed Its Message

Yoga is experiencing a renaissance worldwide. What has brought about this phenomenon?

Classic Hinduism is not missionary minded in the same sense as Christianity. Christian missionaries share their faith and carry on humanitarian work, but Hindu missionaries only proselytize.

This difference is generated by the diametrically opposed beliefs of the two religions. Yogic spirituality aims at enabling an individual to save himself by recognizing he is "God" and thus shortening his reincarnation cycles. But while Hindus seek to win the world to their religion, humanitarian ideas actually conflict with Hinduism's teaching on karma. Karma dictates that one's shortcomings and sufferings are due to what one has done in previous lives. To help people improve themselves through medicine or education is, in essence, to tinker with their karma.

When the British ruled India, they were still part of a Christian commonwealth. The influence of Christianity upon their society caused them to introduce in India the unheard of practice of serving the community by building hospitals and schools. As a result, there are still in India today many community-based programs borrowed from the biblical model of caring for widows, orphans, the sick and the needy.

Hindu purists, however, such as members of VHP and RSS, oppose allowing India's people to follow any other faith and attempts to improve the desperate plight of the poor. To help soften the cruelty of Hinduism, part of its new missionary strategy to reach the West was to market Yoga as a self-realization program that can solve all of life's problems.

But what do Western missionaries of Hinduism look like? Do they dress in saffron robes like the Hare Krishnas? Not at all. Every Yoga teacher in the West has become a missionary of Hinduism, often unwittingly. These 70,000 instructors in more than 20,000 locations across America alone, who teach millions of people Yoga, come from all walks of life.[24]

In addition to the thousands of Yoga instructors, the heads of business corporations, hospitals, and educational facilities are all missionaries to Hinduism as well. These unsuspecting representatives of the Hindu religion—most who would never think of promoting Bible studies or Christian values as a positive alternative in the workplace—are aggressive missionaries for Eastern mysticism today.

These authority figures claim Yoga's benefits include reduction of stress and burnout, and increased concentration and self-confidence for pregnant women, business people, and senior citizens.

Thus, Nike, HBO, Forbes, Apple, and scores of other Fortune 500 companies offer classes on Yoga meditation as a regular employee benefit. Hospitals promote Yoga programs as alternative medical therapy to reduce blood pressure and benefit the heart. YMCAs and YWCAs offer Hatha Yoga as physical education. Health spas adapt Yoga as wellness programs and relaxation techniques, and urban health clubs across the country offer Yoga classes in response to demand. TV presents Yoga as physical fitness exercises. Google.com displays over 100,000,000 pages on the subject of Yoga. A simple search on Amazon.com pulls up some 18,700 books on Yoga. Some outlet store websites, like Target's, offer thousands of Yoga products. It is no wonder that Yoga is nearly a six billion dollar a year industry. How ironic that a belief system that has deeply impoverished so many in India has become such a lucrative trade.

Clearly, the missionary objective to make the ancient philosophy of Hindu Yoga a part of mainstream Western culture has succeeded.

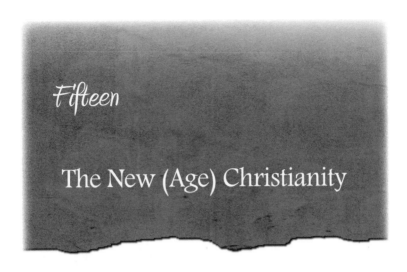

Fifteen

The New (Age) Christianity

The New Age teaches that absolute truth does not exist. Having the Theory of Evolution as a back-up, it claims that all things are ever-changing and developing into other forms; truth, therefore, is based on subjectivity and relativity.

In contrast, God's Word declares that truth is absolute and definable. In fact, *He* is truth and has given man the definition of Himself (Truth) through the Bible, whose writers He inspired.

Proverbs 14:12 warns us that there is a way that seems right to man and appears straight and true but at the end of it is the way of death. A new definition of *Christianity* is being brought forth and heralded as a more relevant, more authentic Christianity—one to which today's postmodern generation can relate. It is important to measure the underlying beliefs of this *new spirituality*, as it is often called, against the truth of God's Word. Those who understand the New Age movement, and more importantly, what the Bible says, will be able to clearly see that this new Christianity isn't biblical Christianity at all, but rather a new (age) Christianity.

The Emerging Church

One of the movements that has been a major catalyst for this new Christianity is the emerging church. Many consider it to be a Christian movement, but when we take a close look at its philosophies, beliefs, and practices, it becomes very evident that it resonates more with the New Age and Hinduism than it does with a Christianity that is grounded in the Word of God.

Some believe that the only problems with the emerging church are centered around methodology issues such as how much lighting to have, the use of candles, informal locations and attire for church services and so forth. To consider only methodology, however, is to be distracted from the true concerns: it is like telling a neighbor that his house needs painting when his house is burning down and his children are inside.

The driving force of the emerging church is essentially a mystical or contemplative spirituality. It is interspiritual, believing that all paths lead to God, and also panentheistic, believing that God, or divinity, is in all things.

This *emerging spirituality*, which ultimately proclaims the divinity of man, has been around since before the serpent said to Eve, "ye shall be as gods" in the Garden of Eden (Genesis 3:5). It first appeared when Lucifer said, "I will be like the most High [God] (Isaiah 14:14).

Alan Jones, Episcopal priest and Dean of Grace Cathedral in San Francisco, resonates with the emerging church. His belief in an interspiritual faith is typical of the new spirituality now permeating the Western world. The "ancient strand of Christianity" to which he refers in the following statement is speaking of mystical spirituality:

[A]nother ancient strand of Christianity teaches that we
are all caught up in the Divine Mystery we call God,
that the Spirit is in everyone, and that there are depths
of interpretation yet to be plumbed . . . At the cathedral
we "break the bread" for those who follow the path of
the Buddha and walk the way of the Hindus.[1]

This statement exemplifies the three major beliefs underlying emerging spirituality: 1. God is in all human beings, which is also called christ-consciousness (panentheism); 2. Truth is relative and needs to be continually redefined ("yet to be plumbed"); 3. All religions are paths to God (interspirituality).

The New Christians—Putting the Word to Rest

Tony Jones is a leader in the emerging church and one of its most influential writers. Both his 2008 book, *The New Christians: Dispatches from the Emergent Frontier*, and his earlier book, *The Sacred Way*, provide insights into the nature of the emerging church. A careful study of this movement will show that it has two earmarks of the New Age movement: embracing of mysticism and rejection of God's Word.

In *The Sacred Way*, Jones openly acknowledges his affinity with mysticism. His chapters on labyrinths, stations of the cross, the silence, centering (mantric) prayer, and more, leave no doubt that Eastern-style mystical prayer practices are an integral element of the emerging church.

As I have stated before in this book, the outcome of entering altered states through the use of mantra meditation is a new spiritual consciousness that is open to both panentheism and interspirituality.

In order to gain a new spiritual outlook that can see beyond the traditional biblical view, one's view of "truth" must be adjusted. Jones' book, *The New Christians,* provides an outline for such an adjustment. One could sum up the recurrent theme of this book thusly: Emergents say they believe in truth, but they define it as something that is always changing and being refined, can never be grasped, and enfolds all beliefs except the ones that insist there is only one truth.

Jones says it is wrong to accept the Bible as true on faith alone, saying that the "conservative" sees "the sacred text of Christianity [as] indubitable, established by an internal and circular reasoning: 'The Bible claims to be God's truth, so therefore it's true.'"[2]

However, given the Bible's proven record of one hundred percent prophetic accuracy, the conservative has already established God's authorship of the Bible. It follows that what is really being said is, *God claims the Bible is true, therefore it is true.* Sadly, Jones has taken refuge in philosophical reasoning, which has absolutely no bearing in disproving the authority of the Scriptures. In fact, much of the inspiration in the birth of the emerging church, as Jones will acknowledge, was through philosophers, many of whom were atheistic. Thus, the emerging church is a blending of philosophical reasoning coupled with the use of mysticism—a combination that has its members in an ever-growing state of searching and confusion.

Jones also believes that the Gospel has been dormant throughout most of history, able to break through "human institutions" only at specific times. He explains:

> And although [the Gospel] has been crusted over for
> eons, it will inevitably find a time and a fissure, an
> opportunity to blast through that crust and explode,
> volcano-like into the atmosphere.[3]

This is the ongoing emerging message by many proponents of the movement: Christianity as we know it today is ineffective and must change. For instance, Rick Warren, popular author of *The Purpose Driven Life,* says that "for the last 100 years, the hands and feet have been amputated, and the church has just been a mouth."[4] If what Jones and Warren are saying were true, it would mean that God had failed to keep His Gospel alive, or at best had been able only to bring it out of dormancy from time to time. This isn't true, as God has always provided a representation of the true Gospel on the earth throughout history through His body of believers and through the Holy Spirit, whom Jesus promised to leave with us.

Emerging church leaders, like Jones, believe that truth—whether negotiable societal and cultural ideologies or essential Christian doctrine—cannot be concretely pinned down, that what is true for today may not be considered true tomorrow. In fact, his belief that Christian doctrine cannot be "written in stone" is really the point he wants to get across. Emergents love the Bible, he says, but they are not going to be so arrogant as to "assume that [their] convictions about God are somehow timeless." To think they are "establishes an imperialistic attitude that has a chilling effect on the honest conversation that's needed for theology to progress."[5]

There is a subtle twisting in this statement that calls arrogance humility and humility arrogance. Real arrogance rejects the truth God has given in His Word. And the *progression of theology* of which Jones speaks is not limited to legitimately debated theology; even the doctrine of atonement cannot be set in stone. Jones says it is "arrogant and a bit deceptive"[6] to suggest there can be any one understanding of atonement. Jones states that to "try to freeze one particular articulation of the gospel, to make it timeless and universally applicable, actually does an injustice to the gospel."[7] Saying we must "refigure our theology,"[8] emergents are "looking for a Christianity that's still exploratory"[9] (flexible). Theology is "temporary" and we "must carry our theologies with an open hand."[10] He sums it up:

> [E]mergents reject metaphors like "pin it down," "in
> a nutshell," "sum it up," and "boil it down" when
> speaking of God and God's Kingdom, for it simply
> can't be done.[11]

Jones says that the moment we think we have truth and theology figured out, "we *cease* being faithful."[12] The Bible is "a companion on the faith journey, not a textbook of proofs," he insists, adding: "Jesus did not have a 'statement of faith.'"[13] In other words, Jesus was just as vague and unsure about truth, atonement, righteousness, and the Gospel as are the emergents. But this is a complete and horrible distortion of Jesus Christ, who spoke with the authority as one who knew exactly what truth is:

> For he taught them as one having authority, and not as the scribes." (Matthew 7:29)

> Howbeit when he, the Spirit of truth, is come, he will guide you into all truth. (John 16:13)

In their search for God, the emergents use "tools of the medieval mystics and the ancient monastics [i.e., contemplative prayer]" and "sources of truth that are external to traditional [biblical] Christianity, be it philosophy or another religious system."[14] And it is in these other religious systems that the New Christians find "truth.":

> In the aftermath of the myth of objectivity [absolute truth], of [faith] and airtight systems, we're left to embrace our subjectivity, to revel in it, for it's only when we accept our own biases that we allow them to be shaped by contrary opinions and biases. One place where this is most poignant is interreligious dialogue.[15]

"Interreligious dialogue" goes hand in hand with rejecting absolute truth. If all is truth and truth cannot be defined or confined (to the Bible), then the next assumption is that all religions point to God. Such a paradigm shift seeks to bring about a *common ground* among all peoples and beliefs.

Most people do not understand that this aspiration to commonality is emanating from the very heart of Satan's plan. His goal is to eradicate the gap between good and evil in man's perceptions so Satan will be either mistaken for God or considered equal to God. He ruthlessly seeks to achieve his objective to be "like the Most High."

As you can see, the ramifications of rejecting the truth revealed in God's Word are staggering.

Interspirituality—the "Fruit" of Mysticism

It was the late Wayne Teasdale who coined the term *interspirituality*, calling it:

> [A] crossing-over boundaries that mysticism makes possible and concrete. The spiritual common ground which exists among the world's religions will be identified, and its theological implications suggested.[16]

New Agers believe that doctrine and theology are obstacles that prevent people from coming together for one common purpose. Mysticism (i.e., meditation and contemplative prayer), they say, is the common element that can unite all religions. According to Teasdale, who believed truth and God could be found outside of the Christian faith, mysticism is the bridge to unity.

Although Teasdale, a Catholic monk, embraced and espoused New Age concepts, his views on bridging all faiths and drawing on "the mystical core of the world's great religious traditions"[17] have spilled over into evangelical Christianity through some very popular Christian figures. Through the *spiritual formation* (contemplative prayer) movement and the emerging church, practices and views that were virtually unheard of in the church twenty years ago are now being accepted and embraced to some degree in nearly every evangelical denomination. Countless Christian colleges, universities, seminaries, ministries, and churches are welcoming the new spirituality, and often without even realizing what they are doing.

As an example, one of Teasdale's books, *The Mystic Heart,*

features a preface written by Beatrice Bruteau, founder of The School for Contemplation. Not only did Bruteau write glowingly of Teasdale's efforts to "bring our religious traditions together,"[18] she believes God is within every human being. In her book, *What We Can Learn from the East*, she makes these assertions:

> We have realized ourselves as the Self that says only I AM, with no predicate following, not "I am a this" or "I have that quality." Only unlimited, absolute I AM"[19]

In the 1950s, Bruteau, a practicing Catholic, was introduced to the teachings of Ramakrishna and later studied at the Ramakrishna Mission in New York City. She became "enthralled by Ramakrishna's philosophy,"[20] saying:

> I loved Vedanta, and I loved the Christian mystics, whom I started reading at the same time. And do you know what they told me in my classes at the Mission? They told me Catholicism was Vedanta in European dress.[21]

Bruteau was an editor for the quarterly journal *American Vedantist* and the author of *The Other Half of My Soul*, a tribute to Catholic monk Bede Griffiths' "blend of Christian belief and Hindu practice."[22]

Despite Bruteau's obvious spiritual affinities, one of today's most popular Christian speakers and authors (a favorite among college students) calls Bruteau a "trustworthy guide to contemplative consciousness."[23] Brennan Manning considers Bruteau "trustworthy" because, as many of his writings prove, he resonates with mysticism and interspirituality.

Manning also commends Bede Griffiths. The late Griffiths is said to have been as much Hindu as he was Catholic and authored at least a dozen books on what he termed Christian-Hindu dialogue. Griffiths interspiritual affinity led him to say:

[O]ur task in India is not so much to bring Christ to India (as though he could be absent), as to discover Christ already present and active in the Hindu soul.[24]

How does Brennan Manning view Griffiths? In two of his books, he quotes Griffiths in a positive manner. And in a conversation at one of Manning's seminars, he said: "I have been reading him [Griffiths] for years going all the way back to *The Golden String* [Griffiths' autobiography written over forty years ago]."[25]

Manning's view on mysticism would be equal to that of Griffiths or Bruteau. This is plain to see when we read what Manning says in his popular book, *The Signature of Jesus*: "the first step in faith is to stop thinking about God at the time of prayer" and "choose a single sacred word . . . repeat the sacred word inwardly, slowly, often."[26]

It is very important to understand—and I hope *Out of India* has helped to show this—that mysticism is the venue in which spirituality takes on the characteristics of the New Age and Hinduism—namely interspirituality (the belief that all paths lead to God) and panentheism (the belief that God is in all).

The very sinister implications of interspirituality are explained in this excerpt from Roger Oakland's refutation of the emerging church, *Faith Undone*:

> The fruit of mysticism is interspirituality. And in that realm where all things are unified and supposedly no separation between man, God, or creation exists, all is welcome . . . except the Cross of Jesus Christ. Rejection of the atonement is where interspirituality ultimately leads. This is where the emerging church is going. . . .
>
> Instead of proclaiming the Gospel of Jesus Christ that saves sinners from hell, a new gospel is being preached, and its preachers are wearing interspiritual robes of deception.[27]

When the Lines are Blurred

The Bible draws very distinct lines around truth. That truth, as presented in both the Old and New Testaments, points explicitly to Jesus Christ and His sacrificial atonement for man. It proclaims that Jesus Christ bore the sins of the world on the Cross, died and rose again, and freely offers salvation to all who accept and believe on Him. It has always been Satan's plan to blur the lines of good and evil and to redefine truth so that he could ultimately receive the same glory that God the Father has bestowed upon Jesus. If he can convince people that man is equal to God and shares His divine attributes, then he can convince man that he does not need a Savior from sin.

Jesus cautioned that many claiming to be Christ and many false prophets will come before He returns. The Bible says that in the last days apostasy will come. Many will turn away from the truth to heed, instead, deceiving spirits and the counterfeit doctrines of demons. It is a comfort to know that God is in control. He warned us of these things, and we know they are an indication of Christ's soon return. At the same time, however, watching deception come into the church is utterly heartbreaking.

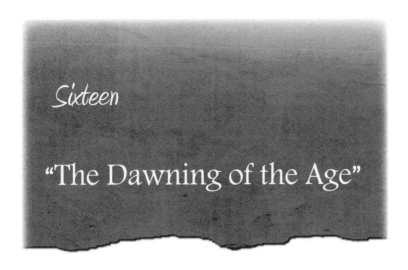

Sixteen

"The Dawning of the Age"

A Conditioning Process

One day in 1979, a young California business man was on his morning jog on a hillside path overlooking the Pacific Ocean. Feeling the breeze against his face and taking in the beauty around him, he suddenly heard a whispered voice within him. He describes the experience:

> It formed into a pair of meaningless but mellifluous-sounding syllables in my mind, which gradually grew into a chant. To the beat of my running steps I gave voice to it, feeling a bursting joy: Kah-lee! ... Kah-lee! Somehow I knew that it was good and right for me to be doing this. Several months later, a friend gave me a copy of Paramahansa Yogananda's *Autobiography of a Yogi*. A few pages into the text, reading the author's account of his early life in India, I came across these words: "Our family moved to Lahore in the Punjab. There I acquired a picture of the Divine Mother in the form of the goddess Kali."

I was stunned. No wonder on that morning run I had felt such an abounding bliss . . . I had been chanting the name of a Nature god! I later learned that on that morning I had been a few hundred yards from the seaside ashram that Yogananda occupied for many years. Many mysterious experiences led me eventually to the feet of this master.[1]

The jogger that day was Jim Ballard, the author of *Mind Like Water*, a primer in Eastern religious practices. Former New Age follower Warren Smith describes his own reaction to Ballard's experience with Kali:

Just as I had not questioned the supernatural circumstances that led me to Indian guru Bhagwhan Shree Rajneesh, Ballard did not question the supernatural circumstances that led him to Paramahansa Yogananda. Yet if either one of us had been seriously reading the Bible back then we might have looked at our spiritual experiences quite differently. . . .

Fueled by his supernatural experience with "Kali" and by other various "mysterious experiences," Ballard was eventually led to "the feet" of Yogananda just as I had been led by my mysterious experiences to "the feet" of Rajneesh.[2]

Ballard's experience took place nearly thirty years ago, but the effect the Hindu god had on him continue. In his book, *Little Wave and Old Swell* (most recently published in 2007), Ballard says the book was "Inspired by [Hindu swami] Paramahansa Yogananda."[3]

Sadly, a very popular Christian figure has written glowing forewords to both of Ballard's books: Ken Blanchard, author of *The One Minute Manager* and founder of "Lead Like Jesus," calls *Mind Like Water* a "wonderful book," adding:

I hope that you and countless other readers will find in *Mind Like Water* some ways to calm your mind and uplift your consciousness, and to transform the way you operate every day in this chaotic world.[4]

Little Wave and Old Swell is a children's book that carries the same message as Helen Schucman's *A Course in Miracles*—a New Age book made popular largely through Oprah Winfrey's promotion. What is the theme of the *Course?*—that man is divine, and God is in all. In the foreword to *Little Wave and Old Swell*, Blanchard tells readers to "[r]ead it many times. Let it speak to your heart."

Blanchard's endorsement of *Mind Like Water* and *Little Wave and Old Swell* is a prime example of how New Age spirituality has entered Christianity.

In view of these things, I cannot help but recall the lyrics I heard so many years ago at the musical *Hair:* "This is the dawning of the Age of Aquarius."[5] But unlike the optimistic, utopian world the hippies in the 1960s thought was in the making, the Bible says the world will enter a time of strong spiritual delusion. Revelation 12: 9 says that at some point in history, before Jesus Christ returns, Satan will deceive the whole world.

Our hope as young hippies, for a world with "Harmony and understanding, Sympathy and trust abounding,"[6] will not occur. True peace will not come before the world experiences a great tribulation, as Revelation describes, but will only occur *after* Jesus Christ comes back to take His rightful place as King. Before Christ returns, the Anti-christ will come, and many will fall into his grip of madness and deceit.

Before the world can accept this world leader, a conditioning process must first take place. Such a process has been going on for some decades. Western society has been heavily influenced and altered by it already, as I have documented in this book. The last hold out against the New Age of Aquarius is the Christian church. Now, that too is caving in under the assault.

Gurus of the West

In writing the first version of this book, titled *Gods of the New Age,* in 1985, I joined many others in sounding a warning: people like Dave Hunt, David Wilkerson, Johanna Michaelsen, and Rabi Maharaj shared the same deep concerns over the impending dangers of Hinduism, the occult, and the New Age movement. But in the last fifteen years or so, it seems that this warning has been falling on deaf ears. Many Christians have come to believe that the New Age died out years ago. The term *New Age* is often considered obsolete, and New Age spirituality is rarely addressed in the pulpits of Christian churches.

But the New Age never died. It has been here all along, infiltrating the fields of education, government, medicine, business, and religion: not one facet of our society has been untainted by it. Often it has crept in subtly, like a painless but deadly cancer going undetected until it is almost too late to stop.

When people hear talk about Hinduism and Eastern gurus, many picture withered old wise men sitting on mountain tops somewhere in India. However, the spirituality of prominent men and women in our Western world is stamped with the influence of India's gurus. In essence, through the teachings of these gurus, these Eastern-influenced leaders have become *gurus of the West.*

Jack Canfield is one such Western guru. His books sit on millions of bookshelves across North America; few people have not heard of Jack Canfield and his *Chicken Soup for the Soul* series. And without a doubt, Christians have been part of the readership embracing his feel-good, positive stories. It is unlikely, however, that very many of these readers know that Canfield is a conduit for the Hindu swamis. Interestingly, the second book of the series, *A 2nd Helping of Chicken Soup for the Soul,* contains a quote by Hindu guru Sai Baba.[7]

In an article in *India Today*, Canfield says that what "works" for him in religion is "a combination of disciplines" that include Yoga, tai chi (a Chinese martial art), and three kinds of meditation: vipasana, transcendental and mantra meditation.[8]

Canfield had a "spiritual awakening" during a Yoga class in college, during which he says, "I knew without any doubt that God existed and flowed through all living things."[9]

In a book Canfield and his co-author Mark Victor Hansen endorse—*Hot Chocolate for the Mystical Soul*, written in the same fashion as their own *Chicken Soup* series—Hinduism is a prevailing theme. On the back cover of the *Hot Chocolate* book Canfield says:

> The remarkable stories in this book . . . will change your beliefs, stretch your mind, open your heart and expand your consciousness.[10]

Canfield and Hansen would hardly be considered counter-culture, fringe-edge New Age hippies. Yet these respected, successful business men hold seminars and reach millions of people with the New Age message. Remember, Canfield was one of the teachers in *The Secret* (see page 172).

Another person who has been influenced by Hindu gurus and has had an impact on Western spirituality is psychiatrist Gerald Jampolsky. In *Teach Only Love*, Jampolsky writes about "an unusual experience with the Indian guru, Swami 'Baba' Muktananda" when attending the guru's ashram.[11] In one of the meetings, Muktananda brushed Jampolsky with a peacock feather, which Jampolsky describes as "an experience that resulted in a radical shift in my belief system."[12] Warren Smith discusses the significance of Jampolsky's spiritual overhaul:

> That next year, 1975, Jampolsky's good friend Judith Skutch, who was soon to become the publisher of *A Course in Miracles*, gave him a copy of the *Course* while it was still in manuscript form. . . .
>
> Jampolsky describes how one day while reading the *Course*, he heard an "inner voice" telling him, "Physician, heal thyself: this is your way home."

Supernaturally impressed by the inner voice and by what he was reading, Jampolsky became an almost immediate convert to the "God" and "Christ" of *A Course in Miracles*. He has been a prominent *A Course in Miracles* proponent and New Age leader ever since.[13]

Smith, in *Deceived on Purpose: The New Age Implications of the Purpose Driven Church*, goes on to describe the connection between Robert Schuller, a highly prolific Christian author and pastor, and Jampolsky. Right about the time that Jampolsky's book *Love is Letting Go of Fear* was introducing Smith to *A Course of Miracles* (which led to his becoming a New Age follower for a number of years), "Schuller was introducing Jampolsky to his *Hour of Power* television audience."[14] Ironically, shortly after Smith's own book on New Age deceptions in the church came out in 2004, Schuller invited Jampolsky back to the Crystal Cathedral and began promoting Jampolsky's 1999 book, *Forgiveness* (with a foreword by New Ager Neale Donald Walsch) on his website.

It is really no wonder that Schuller clicked with someone who had been deeply touched by Hinduism. Marcus Bach writes in *The Unity Way*, that Schuller assured him of "how much Unity principles meant to him and how helpful they had been to him in his work."[15] Bach clarified those principles, writing that: "Hinduism's emphasis on meditation fit[s] well into Unity's patterns for enlightenment."[16]

Global Consciousness

When Jack Canfield talks about expanding "your consciousness," he is talking about the same consciousness as the cosmic consciousness of the Hindu swamis. This consciousness, brought about through meditation, leads to certain philosophical and theological conclusions. First of all, it leads to the belief that God is everything, and everything is God.

Second, due to the boundary-erasing sensations of this altered state of mind, an individual can reach only one political conclusion—that there is no community but global community.

How well I remember my own cosmic excursions. Those experiences powerfully convinced me that I was one with everything—trees, clouds, animals, people, the universe. Because of that deception, I found myself adhering to the global vision shared by virtually all mystics.

A global community will unite all the religions of the world together forming one religious body led by one world leader; eventually, the Bible says, the world will bow down and worship that leader as God.

While there have been religious and political moves toward this global, one-world body through organizations like the United Nations and the World Council of Churches, a great push for unity is now occurring within the scope of Christian denominations. Robert Schuller's autobiography, *My Journey,* includes this statement:

> I met once more with the Grand Mufti [a Muslim], truly one of the great Christ-honoring leaders of faith. . . . I'm dreaming a bold impossible dream: that positive-thinking believers in God will rise above the illusions that our sectarian religions have imposed on the world, and that leaders of the major faiths will rise above doctrinal idiosyncrasies, choosing not to focus on disagreements, but rather to transcend divisive dogmas to work together to bring peace and prosperity and hope to the world.[17]

> [S]tanding before a crowd of devout Muslims with the Grand Mufti, I know that we're all doing God's work together. Standing on the edge of a new millennium, we're laboring hand in hand to repair the breach.[18]

And even though Schuller's "bold impossible dream" in which he believes all religions are "doing God's work" to bring "peace and prosperity and hope to the world" is unbiblical, many Christian leaders have joined together with Schuller. In 2008, Schuller and emerging church pastor Erwin McManus hosted the "Rethink Conference" at the Crystal Cathedral, calling the event an "unprecedented convergence of influential Christian and global leaders."[19] Speakers included Kay Warren (wife of Rick Warren), Gary Smalley, Chuck Colson, Dan Kimball, Lee Strobel, and several other popular Christian leaders.

The influence that mysticism is having in the Christian faith is alarming: global reformation, expansive redemption (all creation being saved), and unity at all costs are just some of the outcomes. It's a no-win situation—the more mysticism is practiced, the stronger these ecumenical, interspiritual leanings become; and the stronger the interspiritual leanings are, the more mysticism is embraced.

A case in point is Rick Warren's Purpose Driven program. Warren talks about breath prayers and Benedictine monks in his book *The Purpose Driven Life*,[20] and has endorsed and promoted Eastern-style meditation proponents like Gary Thomas (*Sacred Pathways*), Leonard Sweet (*Quantum Spirituality*), Ken Blanchard, and the late Henri Nouwen.[21] Warren is the founder of the global P.E.A.C.E. Plan, developed to create what he calls a *three-legged stool* wherein religion, government, and business come together to rid the planet of its diseases, poverty, and other major problems. Warren believes this plan can bring about a "new reformation," but his reformation is one that he says can include Muslims, gays, and virtually anyone.[22]

A dear friend once asked me, "What's wrong with everyone working together? Isn't that a good thing?"

I answered that Christ's Great Commission to His followers, to evangelize the world, didn't consider this to be a criterion. Jesus Christ's last commission to his disciples was to go to all the world and preach the Gospel to every creature (Mark 16:15) teaching them to "observe all things" as Jesus commanded (Matthew 28:19-20), and of course what Jesus taught was based on the prophets, with Himself as that fulfillment.

Paul wrote that Jesus is a stumbling block and foolishness to the unbeliever (I Corinthians 1:23). Jesus warned "wide is the gate, and broad is the way" that leads to destruction, and many shall enter that gate, but "narrow is the way, which leadeth unto life" and "few there be that find it" (Matthew 7:14).

Jesus told his disciples to go out and call people to repentance. But this "new reformation" (that is, the new spirituality) is not calling for repentance and not proclaiming this narrow gate (through Christ) but is rather exalting a wide, all-inclusive road. It is a "reformation" not founded on God's Word and thus a reformation not from Him.

So one can only ask, what is the force behind this global effort to bring all religions together? It can only be one of two things: God or Satan. And the Bible is clear on which it is.

Theosophic beliefs also form a part of the foundation of New Age doctrine. Although the concepts of Theosophy have been around for thousands of years, modern Theosophy was founded by Helena Blavatsky in her book, *The Secret Doctrine.* Blavatsky began her career as a spirit medium. For ten years, she was under the control of a spirit.

Finally, in 1875, she established the Theosophical Society in New York with the help of a gentleman named Colonel Olcott, with whom she later traveled to India. Together they completed the modern Theosophic system by adding elements of Hinduism and Buddhism to it.

Simply put, Theosophy teaches the following: mankind is evolving spiritually. There is one Supreme World Teacher who decides when the world is ready to enter a higher plane of evolution. When this teacher feels the time is right, he looks for a very advanced human being, takes control of his body, and lives in and speaks through that body.

Remarkably, this precisely echoes Satan's plans as disclosed by the Bible.

The Age of Aquarius?

Satan has been working for centuries to bring about this one-world system. He has been unable to do so because God has not permitted it. God is Lord, and "at the time appointed the end shall be" (Daniel 8:19). Daniel had a vision that would take place "at the time of the end" (vs. 17):

> [A] king of fierce countenance, and understanding dark sentences, shall stand up.
>
> And his power shall be mighty, but not by his own power: and he shall destroy wonderfully, and shall prosper, and practise, and shall destroy the mighty and the holy people.
>
> And through his policy also he shall cause craft to prosper in his hand; and he shall magnify himself in his heart, and by peace shall destroy many. (Daniel 8:23-25)

The prophet Jeremiah spoke of a time when people would declare peace, but there would be no peace (Jeremiah 6:14).

The apostle Paul issued this warning in I Thessalonians 5:3:

> For when they shall say, Peace and safety; then sudden destruction cometh upon them, as travail upon a woman with child; and they shall not escape.

According to New Agers, a *peaceable* end-time Utopia will be ushered in by a World Teacher. He will unite mankind into economic, political, and religious unity.

Bible-believing Christians know that just such a world leader is coming, and that this leader will not be Jesus Christ, but a false christ. Scripture predicts it. In II Thessalonians 2:3 it says:

> Let no man deceive you by any means: for that day

shall not come, except there come a falling away first,
and that man of sin be revealed, the son of perdition.

The dark horrific days of the Great Tribulation won't come
until great numbers of professing Christians turn away from
the true Gospel and the evil world leader is revealed, the son
of destruction, who will stand in opposition to every deity and
exalt himself above every god. Eventually, he will take his seat in
God's temple at Jerusalem, and declare himself to be the God of
the universe.

Altered states of consciousness, Yoga, contemplative prayer,
martial arts, Reiki—all of these are clearly preparing man for the
entrance of Satan's leading actor upon history's stage, the one whom
the Bible calls "that man of sin" (II Thessalonians 2:3).

An Enlightened Race?

The Germany of the 1920s and 1930s was in social and economic despair, looking for a leader who would free her from the
Great Depression. The man with the promise of hope was Adolph
Hitler. A man with an affinity for the occult and "an abiding belief
in astrology,"[23] he claimed he was ordained by God to usher in
one thousand years of peace and prosperity with a super race of
humans. A student of Blavatsky's *The Secret Doctrine* (the Theosophical Society's "bible"), Hitler manipulated an entire nation
to surrender its collective mind to him.[24]

Aryanism, the belief in a super-race, is a foundational teaching
of Hinduism's caste system. It was also Hitler's twisted rationale for
the annihilation of six million Jews and additional millions of other
"impure" racial and societal strains. This same attitude of elitism
breeds the New Age viewpoint of man's coming "quantum leap in
the evolution of consciousness" that will create a new "awakened"
and "enlightened" race.[25] But there won't be any room for those
who resist this transformed mystical world.

Gurus excuse away the madness and cruelty of the Holocaust
as being the result of inadequate karma. Even Gandhi pleaded

with the British to surrender to Hitler. "Hitler is not a bad man," he told them.[26]

Neale Donald Walsch, in one of his popular *Conversations with God* books, said God told him the following:

> I do not love "good" more than I love "bad." Hitler went to heaven. When you understand this, you will understand God.[27]

> Hitler didn't hurt anyone. In a sense, he didn't inflict suffering, he ended it.[28]

> The mistakes Hitler made did no harm or damage to those whose deaths he caused. Those souls were released from their earthly bondage, like butterflies emerging from a cocoon.[29]

I find it astounding that even though Walsch made such statements, his *Conversations with God* books remained on the *New York Times* Best Seller List for over two years, selling millions of copies. While most people would say that what happened in Germany under Hitler was an atrocity that must never be repeated, the New Age is conditioning people toward the same mindset. Those who refuse to be enlightened or awakened (to the divinity within) stand in the way of the world's healing and need to be removed. Barbara Marx Hubbard, a prolific New Age author and speaker, calls this the *selection process*.[30]

To Westerners, the swastika symbolizes Nazism, but to the Hindu, it is a very familiar symbol of power, still seen today in many Indian temples. In true New Age spirit, the Fuhrer saw himself as a global leader and adopted it. In his madness for world power and domination, Hitler stated:

> I had to encourage "national" feelings for reasons of expediency; but I was already aware that the "nation" idea could only have a temporary value. The

The Hindu Swastika

day will come when even here in Germany what is known as "nationalism" will practically have ceased to exist. What will take its place in the world will be a universal society of masters and overlords.[31]

Most people don't think of Hitler as a New Ager or certainly not a Hindu, but his philosophy on the "divinity" of man was right in line with the pantheistic view:

> A new variety of man is beginning to separate out. The old type of man will have but a stunted existence. All creative energy will be concentrated in the new one. . . . I might call the two varieties [of man] the god-man and the mass animal. . . . Man is becoming God—that is the simple fact. Man is God in the making.[32]

If virtually an entire country in the 1930s could be deceived and mesmerized by Adolph Hitler, how much more vulnerable is our generation—a generation that has embraced mysticism and New Age philosophy so willingly?

As a young woman, Diet Eman joined the Dutch resistance movement during World War II. In her compelling true story, *Things We Couldn't Say,* she makes an interesting comparison between the Dutch and German people at that time:

> [T]he Dutch have a long tradition of thinking for themselves, not just swallowing what officials tell them. They have a tradition of not being merely followers, as the Germans seemed to me to be. Our not following orders made life difficult for the Germans, more difficult than they had thought it

would be. They had to treat us as if they were balancing on a tightrope. A German named Seyss-Inquart, the Nazi in charge of the Netherlands, tried to convince us that we belonged to the great Aryan race and that we should be overjoyed that we'd been accepted. But, quite simply, many Dutch people never followed orders.[33]

I see many similarities in the United States, and in the Western world at large, to German society in the 1930s. Christians by the carloads rush from one conference to another to learn about community, leadership, small groups, and the like. But I propose that what they are getting isn't training to be good leaders but rather subtle induction to being good *followers*, lulled to lay aside independent thinking. "Follow, follow, follow!" chants the chorus of today's leaders, all the while singing the praises of Eastern concepts and mystical practices. Our way of thinking—and not thinking—is being radically altered, and the majority of people, including Christians, don't even see what is happening.

A Paradigm Shift

Dean Ornish, whom I discussed in an earlier chapter, made an interesting observation about his spiritual mentor-guru:

> Swami Satchidananda was once asked, "What's the difference between illness and wellness?'" He walked over to a blackboard [during Grand Rounds at the University of Virginia Medical Center] and wrote illness and circled the first letter, i. He then wrote wellness and circled the first two letters, we.[34]

That may sound noble at first. But the New Age emphasis on the collective "we" as opposed to the individual "I" is actually an intolerance for what they call "self-centeredness"—any belief that is exclusive and claims to be the only way. Listen to this thought-provoking explanation:

In the near future established religions may still retain
the general nature of their individual identities. But
. . . a "self-centered" and "exclusivistic" belief in a
personal Savior would not be conducive to a world
seeking peace and harmony. In other words . . . in
the days of the New Spirituality, Jesus can be your
friend but *not* your Lord and Savior. In a statement
that should sober every Christian believer on the
face of the earth, [Neale Donald] Walsch's "God"
warned: "Yet let me make something clear. The era of
the Single Savior is over. What is needed now is joint
action, combined effort, collective co-creation."[35]

Interestingly, Rick Warren talks about "self-centeredness" in
The Purpose Driven Life and connects it to a mystical practice.
In chapter 38 titled "Becoming a World-Class Christian," Warren
says that Christians must "[s]hift from self-centered thinking to
other-centered thinking."[35] Warren says that such a feat cannot be
done on our own strength and suggests that "breath prayers" be
used to help. He discusses this kind of prayer earlier in the book
in a chapter where he tells readers that these repetitive "breath
prayers" help "counteract wandering thoughts" (a common goal
with all mantra mediators).[36] Warren refers to a mystic monk
named Brother Lawrence who "danced violently like a mad-man"
when he "practiced the presence of God" as he called it.[37]

Some may say that Rick Warren isn't intentionally relating
this idea of "self-centeredness" to mysticism. That may or may
not be true, but nevertheless, the point I want to make is that
the paradigm shift toward *community salvation* as opposed to
individual salvation through a personal relationship with Jesus
Christ (the end of the "era of the Single Savior") is occurring
right now, and to see Rick Warren, who *Time* magazine recently
called "America's most powerful religious leader,"[38] tell millions
that they can rid themselves of "self-centeredness" by way of an
eastern-style prayer method is very troubling.

In 2005, Rick Warren told his congregation that Ken Blanchard had "signed on" to help implement Warren's global P.E.A.C.E. Plan.[39] Considering Blanchard's endorsement of *Little Wave and Old Swell*, the book inspired by Hindu swami Paramahansa Yogananda, it is not exaggerated to predict that Hinduistic spirituality will have a heightened role in the future of this new Christianity.

Counterfeits Versus the Real Thing

I didn't write *Out of India* to criticize India or the people of India. I love that country, and I especially love its people. My greatest hope is that many, many people of India will come to know the truth of the Gospel of Jesus Christ. Sadly, the same darkness I see in millions of people there, I see in Europe and North America as well. An unprecedented spiritual blindness is pervading western culture at large like never before. Those who have had the fullest revelation of Light are rejecting it and turning to darkness. This book is a call to the Christian who has turned away from a biblical true faith, to repent; and it is a plea to unbelievers to surrender to Jesus Christ, the Lord God.

The devil hasn't changed his tactics since the Garden of Eden. Satan is described in the Bible as the father of lies (John 8:44). He is a counterfeiter. Virtually every trait or characteristic of the false religious systems he has given to the world is a poor substitute for some aspect of biblical Christianity. The coming "Messiah" he is promising is not the resurrected Jesus.

New Age practices and philosophies have been infiltrating our society for decades. In this millennium, however, these deceptions are spreading exponentially. They are advanced through DVDs, magazines, and books, such as Schucman's *A Course in Miracles* and Eckhart Tolle's *A New Earth,* both promoted by Oprah.[40] They are spread in the church through contemplative spirituality and the emerging church in denominations worldwide. The objective of these deceptions is to dismantle biblical doctrine and replace it with "seducing spirits, and doctrines of devils" (I Timothy 4:1).

The leaders who teach a New Age Christianity use Scripture to support many of their ideas, and advocate practices, which can appear, on the surface, biblically sound. Careful examination of their teachings, however, shows that these leaders are twisting the meaning of Scripture to suit their own ends, just as Satan has always done.

"For the mystery of iniquity doth already work," Paul warns in his second letter to the Thessalonian church; "only he who now letteth [restrains] will let, until he be taken out of the way. And then shall that Wicked be revealed" (2:7,8).

In the meantime, it is belief in our personal God, the mighty Creator, that stands against the lies of occultism, witchcraft, and the New Age. It is the finished work of Jesus Christ that eclipses the feeble philosophies of man. It is the unlimited power of the Holy Spirit that confronts the lesser powers of Satan, even though the latter performs signs and wonders.

And it is a commitment to the Bible as God's complete, accurate revelation to man that ends the perpetual search for greater enlightenment, for unity, for self-realization. As we submit to God's Spirit and immerse ourselves in His Word, He will do His work. He will keep us alert and reveal the counterfeits.

Spiritual counterfeits are like rat poison, which contains .005 per cent poison mixed into 99.995 per cent wholesome food. Rats and mice do not detect the miniscule, but deadly, poison. The deceptions of Hinduism were too obvious for even unbelievers in the Western world to accept, so they were repackaged as New Age teachings. Now, these teachings have been mixed with biblical truth and dressed in Christian labels producing a spiritual poison. The result? Satan's clever counterfeits are being swallowed up by Christians everywhere.

A friend of mine, Chris, approached me one day: "Mum's been working at the bank for over a year," she told me. "And she's been getting the most amazing education."

"What do you mean?"

"She's learning all about money."

"I guess she'd have to know about money if she's going to work in a bank." I laughed.

Chris smiled. "I mean she's *really* learning about money. They're teaching her the color of each bill, the size of it, even the way it's watermarked. They're showing her the details of the inks and papers."

"How do they teach her?"

"Well, they just keep having her handle it. They point out all the various things they want her to remember. But they figure the more she works with money, feels it, counts it, and stacks it, the more familiar it'll be to her."

"That makes sense, I suppose. But what's the point?"

"Here's the point. Yesterday they blindfolded her. Then they slipped a couple of counterfeit bills in her stack of money. She picked them out by touch!"

"It's been proven a thousand times over that if a bank teller knows the real money extremely well, he can't be fooled by the counterfeits."

More valuable than all the money in the world are the treasures of the Spirit. And every precious facet of God's kingdom has its pseudo-counterpart in the world, the flesh, or the devil.

Just as bank tellers steadily become more familiar with money, so we need to steadily become more familiar with the Bible. And, because of the increasingly cunning deceptions of Satan, we need to steadily become more familiar with the whole counsel of God (Acts 20:27), to learn what a verse or passage means in the context of the rest of the Bible. Jesus said that those who hear His words and do them will be like a wise man who built his house on a rock. When the rain, winds, and floods came and beat upon the house, it did not fall (Matthew 7:24-25). His Word is our best defense against the tsunamis of deception beating upon the world and the church.

Unfortunately, like so many others, I became acquainted with the counterfeits first. I blindly enveloped myself in counterfeit love. I soared on wings of counterfeit power. I stood proud and arrogant in my own, but counterfeit, strength. And I dreamily dozed through years of counterfeit peace.

Then, like the blazing sun breaking through the clouds after a long stretch of foggy days, Jesus entered my life. The counterfeits vanished, burned away by His truth through His mercy and grace. How desperately I had needed Him before I had even understood who He was!

Now my greatest longing is to tell those who are lost in that same darkness of Christ's free gift of salvation through His amazing grace. I long to share the news of His forgiveness, to proclaim His faithfulness, and to see others rejoice in His lovingkindness.

I long most of all to warn those who are searching, just as I was, of the dangers they face. The most cleverly devised, brilliantly packaged counterfeits are yet to come. The coming world ruler and his evil world system will some day emerge. The best words of caution I can possibly offer are the words of Jesus Himself:

> Take heed that no man deceive you. For many shall come in my name, saying, I am Christ; and shall deceive many. (Matthew 24:4,5)

> Then if any man shall say unto you, Lo, here is Christ, or there; believe it not. For there shall arise false Christs, and false prophets, and shall shew great signs and wonders; insomuch that, if it were possible, they shall deceive the very elect. (Matthew 24:23-24)

> I am the way, the truth, and the life: no man cometh unto the Father, but by me. (John 14:6)

Endnotes

1/Bus Ride to the Future

1. "You Can Walk Across it on the Grass" (*Time* magazine, April 15, 1966, http://www.time.com/time/printout/0,8816,835349,00.html), cover story.

2. A musical, written by James Rado, Galt Macdermot, and Gerome Ragni, first opening at opening in New York at the Biltmore Theatre on West 47th Street in 1968.

3. "Where Do I Go?," song in the production, *Hair*. All Rights Reserved. Used with permission of ALFRED PUBLISHING CO., INC. (see Lyric Credits, p. 232).

4. William Shakespeare, *Halmet* (Courier Dover Publications, 1992 edition written around 1600), p. 42.

5. "Let the Sunshine In," song in the production, *Hair*.

6. "Walking in Space," song in the production, *Hair*. All Rights Reserved. Used with permission of ALFRED PUBLISHING CO., INC. (see Lyric Credits, p. 232).

7. "Aquarius," song in the production, Hair. All Rights Reserved. Used with permission of ALFRED PUBLISHING CO., INC. (see Lyric Credits, p. 232).

8. Marilyn Ferguson, *The Aquarian Conspiracy* (Los Angeles, CA: J. P. Tarcher, Inc., 1980), p. 19.

9. David Spangler, *Emergence* (Delta 1984), p. 17.

5/Landing in the Butter

1. Poem by Caryl Matrisciana.

10/In the Land of the Guru

1. Upasana Bhat, "Prostitution 'increases' in India" (*BBC News*, Delhi, July 3, 2006, http://news.bbc.co.uk/2/hi/south_asia/5140526.stm).

2. Robert I. Friedman, "India's Shame: Sexual Slavery and Political Corruption Are Leading to An AIDS Catastrophe" (*The Nation*, Vol. 262, No. 14, New York, April 8, 1996).

3. Central Board of Film Certification (Government of India, http://www.cbfcindia.tn.nic.in).

4. G.B. Singh, *Gandhi: Behind the Mask of Divinity* (Prometheus Books, 2004), p. 76.

5. "Population of India," from http://www.indianchild.com/population_of_india.htm.

6. List of countries by GDP (nominal): taken from http:// en.wikipedia.org/wiki/List_of_countries_by_GDP_(nominal), the CIA's *World Factbook* for 2007.

7. "Work Among Children" (South Asian Council for Community and Children in Crisis, http://www.sac-ccc.org/2006/index.php?option=com_content&task=view&id=16&Itemid=33).

8. Ibid.

9. Richard Grenier, "The Gandhi Nobody Knows" ("Commentary," March 1983, published monthly by the American Jewish Committee, New York, NY, http://history.eserver.org/ghandi-nobody-knows.txt).

10. Quote by Satyananda Saraswati, accessed at http://www.7centers.com/10daytransformation.html.

11. The Gura Gita passages, accessed at: http://www.srinannagaru.com/articles/gurugita/gurugita.pdf.

12. Michael Ray, *Creativity in Business* (Garden City, NY: Doubleday & Co., Inc, 1986, 1st Edition), back flap.

13. Michael Ray, *The Highest Goal* (San Francisco, CA: Berrett-Koehler Publishers, Inc., 2004), p. 28.

14. Michael Ray, *Creativity in Business*, op. cit., p. 37.

15. Elizabeth Gilbert, quotes from Oprah Winfrey's website: http://www.oprah.com/slideshow/oprahshow/slideshow1_ss_20071005_350/6.

16. Ibid.

17. Ibid.

18. Ibid.

19. Philip St. Romain, *Kundalini Energy and Christian Spirituality* (Crossroad Pub. Co., 1995), p. 39.

20. Anne Lamott, on the back cover of *Eat, Pray, Love* by Elizabeth Gilbert.

11/Two Aquarian Fairs—East and West

1. Adapted from: "Meditation by His Holiness Maharishi Mahesh Yogi with Questions and Answers" (*International SRM Publications*, London 1967), p. 140 ff.

2. "Human Suffering & An Unjust God": A conversation between Srila Prabhupada and social worker Ashok Chugani in Bombay (http://www.sivaramaswami.com/?p=2341).

3. From Vishwa Hindu Parishad website: http://www.vhp.org.

4. Ibid.

5. Upper Parramatta River Catchment Education Resource Kit: E5 - Ganges River, Varanasi, (2002, http://www.uprct.nsw.gov.au/PDF/

Info%20Sheets/Enviro%20Issues/E5%20River%20Ganga%20Varanasi%20India.pdf).

6. George Tyler Miller, *Living in the Environment: Principles, Connections, and Solutions* (Thomson Brooks/Cole, 2004, http://tinyurl.com/6q2fav) p. 497.

7. Taken from a brochure at the Mind, Body, Spirit Festival.

8. Swami Sivananda, "Passing Moments in Eternity," Sept. 1970, pp. 14-15. (Taken from Ted Montgomery, *Creation . . . Counterfeits . . . and the 70th Week*, chapter 9, http://www.tedmontgomery.com/bblovrvw/C_9d.html).

9. "Indian Astrology vs. Indian Science" (*BBC World Service*, London, May 31, 2001, http://www.bbc.co.uk/worldservice/sci_tech/highlights/010531_vedic.shtml).

10. Ibid.

11. Alice Bailey, *The Externalization of the Hierarchy* (Albany, NY: Fort Orange Press, Inc., 1972, 4th printing (paperback), p. 597.

12. Larry DeBruyn, "The Music and the Mystical" (August 7, 2006, http://www.frbaptist.org/bin/view/Ptp/PtpTopic20060807151859).

13. Rob Bell, *Velvet Elvis* (Grand Rapids, MI: Zondervan, 2005), p. 72.

14. Larry DeBruyn, op. cit.

12/To Make Men Whole

1. Marilyn Ferguson, *The Aquarian Conspiracy* (Los Angeles, CA: J. P. Tarcher, 1980), p. 419.

2. Ibid., pp. 257-259.

3. Judith Boice, *Menopause with Science and Soul* (Berkeley, CA: Celestial Arts; 1st edition, 2007), p. 125.

4. Andrea Calcano Cruz, "The Oneness Blessing: Helping the Planetary Shift in consciousness" (*Natural Awakenings*, October 2007, http://www.onenessmovementflorida.org/Article%20for%20Michael.pdf).

5. Ibid.

6. Ibid.

7. Mary Anne McPherson Oliver, *Conjugal Spirituality* (Kansas City, MO: Sheed & Ward, 1994), p. 18.

8. Ibid., p. 109.

9. Ibid., p. 27.

10. Douglas Todd, "Sex Brings Christians Closer to God" (*Vancouver Sun*, Saturday, July 26, 2008).

11. Ibid.

12. Chuck M. MacKnee, "Peak Sexual and Spiritual Experiences" (*Sage*

Publications, Theology Sexuality 1996; 3; 97, see online edition: http://tse.sagepub.com/cgi/content/abstract/3/5/97), p. 2.

13. Ibid., p. 4.

14. Wahkeena Sitka Tidepool Ripple, "Can Sex Work Be Shamanic?" (*Alternatives*, Winter 06, Issue 40).

15. Ray Yungen, *For Many Shall Come in My Name* (Eureka, MT: Lighthouse Trails Publishing, LLC, 2nd ed., 2007), p. 113.

16. Martin and Diedre Bobgan, *Hypnosis: Medical, Scientific, or Occultic* (Santa Barbara, CA: Eastgate Publishers, 2001, online edition: http://www.psychoheresy-aware.org/e-books/Hypnosis-ebk.pdf), pp. 87-88, 100.

17. Ibid., p. 130.

18. Dean Ornish, *Program for Reversing Heart Disease* (New York, NY: Ballantine Books, First Ballantine Books Edition, September 1991), Acknowledgements, p. xvii.

19. Ibid., p. 143.

20. Ibid., p. 234.

13/Quest for the Higher Self

1. Shakti Gawain, *Creative Visualization* (Novato, CA: Nataraj Publishing, 2002 edition), p. 97.

2. Ibid., p. 167.

3. Ibid.

4. Norman Vincent Peale, *Positive Imaging* (Ballantine Books, First Ballantine Books Trade Edition, 1996), pp. 28-29.

5. Kimberly Hayes Taylor, "'Secret' spreads around world" (*The News & Observer*, February 2, 2007, http://www.newsobserver.com/105/story/538825.html).

6. Ibid.

7. Ibid.

8. Ibid.

9. "The Secret - Just Do It! Your Wish Is My Command" (Trailer can be viewed at: http://www.youtube.com/watch?v=O9siAkJsUaY).

10. Ray Yungen, *For Many Shall Come in My Name* (Woodburn, OR: Solid Rock Books, Inc., 1991, 1st Edition, Revised), pp. 14-15.

11. Ray Yungen, *For Many Shall Come in My Name*, op., cit., p. 12.

12. Abraham-Hicks Publications, http://www.abraham-hicks.com/lawofattractionsource/about_us.php.

13. Publisher synopsis for "The Moses Code" (April 27, 2008, http://

www.decouvertesetculture.ch/images/codemoeng.doc).

14. Ibid.

15. This trailer was initially on www.youtube.com but was removed shortly after it appeared. Lighthouse Trails editors spoke with personnel for *The Moses Code* on March 3, 2008 and was told the trailer was edited. The new trailer omitted the I AM statements. However, both the book and the DVD contain the "I AM" references.

16. James Twyman, *The Moses Code* (Hay House, 2008, 1ˢᵗ edition), p. 191.

17. Ibid., p. 193.

18. Marilyn Ferguson, *The Aquarian Conspiracy*, op. cit., p. 374.

19. For a well-documented analysis of the contemplative prayer movement, read *A Time of Departing* by Ray Yungen.

20. Richard Foster, *Celebration of Discipline* (San Francisco, CA: Harper & Row, 1978 edition), p. 13.

21. Richard Foster, *Celebration of Discipline* (UK: Hodder and Stoughton, 1980), p. 13.

22. Richard Foster/Renovare, *Spiritual Classics* (San Francisco, CA: HarperCollins, 2000, First Edition), p. 155.

23. John Main, Laurence Freeman, John Main: Essential Writings (Maryknoll, NY: Orbis Books, October 2004, Third Printing), p. 26.

24. Ibid.

25. Daniel Goleman, *The Meditative Mind* (New York, NY: Jeremy Tarcher/Putnam, 1988), p. 53.

14/Yoga Uncoiled

1. "A Growing Profession: 70,000 Yoga Teachers Estimated by NAMASTA North American Studio Alliance (NAMASTA press resources, April 12, 2005, http://www.namasta.com/pressresources.php).

2. "Yoga Journal Releases 2008 'Yoga in America' Market Study," http://www.yogajournal.com/advertise/press_releases/10.

3. "Yoga Health Foundation announces YOGA MONTH 09.2008 national awareness campaign and 10 City Yoga Health Festival Tour," February 1, 2008, http://www.yogamonth.org/yoganews.php.

4. "Yoga Journal Releases 2008 'Yoga in America' Market Study," op. cit.

5. Thomas Keating, *Open Mind, Open Heart* (New York, NY: The Continuum International Publishing Group, Inc., 1986, 1992, 2006); these terms are used throughout Keating's book.

6. Lisa Takeuchi Cullen/Mahtomedi, "Stretching for Jesus (*Time* maga-

zine, August 29, 2005).

7. *Yoga Uncoiled: from east to west* (Menifee, CA: Caryl Productions, 2007).

8. Ibid.

9. Ibid.

10. "Stretching for Jesus," op. cit.

11. Ibid.

12. Ibid.

13. Rabi Maharaj, *Death of a Guru* (Eugene, OR: Harvest House Publishers, 1984 edition).

14. Darryl E. Owens, "'Christian yoga' strikes a new pose" (*Denver Post*, Thursday, May 18, 2006).

15. "Yoga and Meditation," from the Sanatan Society dedicated to the teachings of the late Harish Johari: http://www.sanatansociety.org/yoga_and_meditation/yoga.htm.

16. Ibid.

17. Ibid., "Chakras," http://www.sanatansociety.org/chakras/chakras.htm.

18. Ibid.

19. *Yoga Uncoiled: from east to west*, op. cit., quoting George Alexander.

20. Ibid., quoting Cindy Senarighi.

21. Ibid., quoting George Alexander.

22. *Smith's Bible Dictionary*, http://www.bible-history.com/smiths/D/Divination.

23. *Yoga Uncoiled: from east to west*, op. cit., quoting George Alexander.

24. "A Growing Profession: 70,000 Yoga Teachers Estimated by NAMASTA, North American Studio Alliance," op. cit.

15/ The New (Age) Christianity

1. Alan Jones, *Reimagining Christianity* (Hoboken, NJ: John Wiley & Sons, Inc., 2005), p. 89.

2. Tony Jones, *The New Christians* (San Francisco, CA: Jossey-Bass, a Wiley Imprint, 2008), p. 19.

3. Ibid., p. 36.

4. Paul Nussbaum, "A Global Ministry of 'Muscular Christianity'" (*Washington Post*, January 21, 2006; B09, http://www.washingtonpost.com/wp-dyn/content/article/2006/01/21/AR2006012100284_pf.html, accessed 8/2008).

5. Tony Jones, *The New Christians*, op. cit., p. 114.

6. Ibid., p. 77.

7. Ibid., p. 96.

8. Ibid., p. 104.

9. Ibid., p. 108.

10. Ibid., p. 114.

11. Ibid.

12. Ibid., p. 168.

13. Ibid., p. 234.

14. Ibid., p. 159.

15. Ibid., p. 155.

16. Wayne Teasdale, "Mysticism as the Crossing of Ultimate Boundaries: A Theological Reflection" (*The Golden String* newsletter, Bede Griffiths, Vol. 5, No. 2).

17. Wayne Teasdale, *The Mystic Heart* (Novato, CA: New World Library, 2001), back cover.

18. Ibid., p. xii.

19. An interview with Beatrice Bruteau, "A Song That Goes On Singing" (*What is Enlightenment?* magazine, Issue 21/Spring–Summer 2002, http://www.wie.org/j21, accessed 8/2008).

20. Ibid.

21. Ibid.

22. Beatrice Bruteau, *The Other Half of My Soul: Bede Griffiths and the Hindu-Christian Dialogue* (Wheaton, IL: Theosophical Publishing House, First Quest Edition, 1996), publisher's description of book.

23. Brennan Manning, *Abba's Child* (Colorado Springs, CO: Nav-Press, 1994), p. 180.

24. Bede Griffiths, *Christ in India* (Springfield, IL: Templegate Publishers, 1966), p. 217.

25. At a meeting in Salem, Oregon, Brennan Manning told this to Ray Yungen.

26. Brennan Manning, *The Signature of Jesus* (Sisters, OR: Multnomah, 1996, Revised Edition, 1996), pp. 212, 218.

27. Roger Oakland, *Faith Undone* (Silverton, OR: Lighthouse Trails Publishing, LLC, 2007, 1st edition), pp. 104, 184.

16/ The Dawning of the Age

1. Jim Ballard, *Mind Like Water* (Hoboken, NJ: John Wiley & Sons, 2002), p. 14.

2. Warren Smith, *Reinventing Jesus Christ*, chapter 5 updates: http://www.reinventingjesuschrist.com, p. 12.

3. Jim Ballard, *Little Wave and Old Swell* (New York, NY: Atria Books, Simon & Schuster, Inc., 2007), front cover.

4. Ken Blanchard quoted from foreword of Jim Ballard's *Mind Like Water*, op. cit.,

5. "Aquarius," song in the production, *Hair*, op. cit. (see Lyric

credits, p. 232).

6. Ibid.

7. Jack Canfield, Mark Victor Hansen, *A 2ⁿᵈ Helping of Chicken Soup for the Soul* (Deerfield Beach, FL: Health Communications, Inc., 1995), p. 1.

8. Jack Canfield, "Choosing to be Happy" (*India Today Plus*, 1997).

9. Jack Canfield, Mark Victor Hansen, *Dare to Win* (New York, NY: Berkley Books, Berkley trade paperback edition, 1996), p. 195.

10. Arielle Ford, *Hot Chocolate for the Mystical Soul* (New York, NY: Penguin Group, First Printing, February 1998), back cover.

11. Gerald Jampolsky, *Teach Only Love* (Hillsboro, OR: Beyond Words Publishing, Inc., 2000), p. 18.

12. Ibid., p. 19.

13. Warren Smith, *Deceived on Purpose* (Magalia, CA: Mountain Stream Press, 2ⁿᵈ edition), pp. 44-45.

14. Ibid., p. 67.

15. Ray Yungen, *A Time of Departing*, (Eureka, MT: Lighthouse Trails Publishing, LLC, 2ⁿᵈ ed, 2007), p. 48, citing Marcus Bach, *The Unity Way* (Unity Village, MO: Unity School of Christianity, 1982), p. 267.

16. Ibid.

17. Robert Schuller, *My Journey: From an Iowa Farm to a Cathedral of Dreams* (San Francisco, CA: HarperCollins, First Edition, 2001), p. 502.

18. Ibid., p. 501.

19. Rethink Conference promotional website: http://www.tsnn.com/profile.asp?EventID=23844&CatID=97, accessed 8/2008

20. Rick Warren, *The Purpose Driven Life* (Grand Rapids, MI: Zondervan publishing, 2002), p. 89.

21. For extensive research on Rick Warren's Purpose Driven program and other relevant topics, please go to Lighthouse Trails Research Project: http://www.lighthousetrailsresearch.com.

22. "Rick Warren Distorts the Instructions of Jesus to Fit His Global Peace Plan" (Lighthouse Trails Research Special Report, based on interview between Rick Warren and Charlie Rose, http://www.lighthousetrailsresearch.com/newsletter082506.htm#article1, accessed 8/2008. To view interview: http://video.google.com/videoplay?docid=-5555324196046364882, accessed 8/2008).

23. William Shirer, *The Rise and Fall of the Third Reich* (New York NY: Simon & Schuster, First Touchstone edition, 1981), p. 837.

24. Paul and Phillip Collins, *The Ascendancy of the Scientific Dictatorship* (Book Surge, LLC, 2006), p. 86.

25. Eckhart Tolle, *The Power of Now* (Novato, CA: New World Library and Vancouver, BC: Namaste Publishing, First paperback printing,

2004), p. 67; terms "awakened" and "enlightened" throughout book.

26. Richard Grenier, "The Gandhi Nobody Knows," op. cit.

27. Neale Donald Walsch, *Conversations with God*, Book 1 (New York, NY: Penguin Putnam, First Hardcover edition, 1996), p. 61.

28. Neale Donald Walsch, *Conversations with God,* Book 2 (Charlottesville, VA: Hampton Road Publishing Company, 1997), p. 56.

29. Ibid., p. 42.

30. For more information on Barbara Marx Hubbard's "selection process," read Warren Smith's *Reinventing Jesus Christ* (Conscience Press) online at www.reinventingjesuschrist.com.

31. Jim Keith, *Casebook on Alternative 3* (Lilbum, GA: IllumiNet Press, 1994), p. 151.

32. Hermann Rauschning, *Hitler Speaks* (Kessinger Publishing, LLC, 2006), p.p. 241-242.

33. Diet Eman, *Things We Couldn't Say* (Silverton, OR: Lighthouse Trails Publishing, LLC, 2008), p. 126.

34. Dean Ornish in *The Oprah Magazine,* November 2002, taken from the Sri Swami Satchidananda website: http://swamisatchidananda.org/docs2/health.htm, accessed 8/2008.

35. Warren Smith, *Deceived on Purpose*, op. cit., pp. 61-62.

36. Rick Warren, *The Purpose Driven Life*, op. cit., p. 299.

37. Ibid., p. 88.

38. Brother Lawrence, *The Practice of the Presence of God*, translated by John Delaney, (New York, NY: Doubleday, Image Books, 1977), p. 34.

39. David Van Biema, "The Global Ambition of Rick Warren" (*Time* magazine, August 7, 2008).

40. In November of 2003, in a sermon by Rick Warren at Saddleback Church, Rick Warren states that Ken Blanchard has "signed on" to help with Warren's global P.E.A.C.E. Plan, http://www.lighthousetrailsresearch.com/pressreleasevideoclip.htm.

Photograph and Illustration Credits

1/Bus Ride to the Future

p. 14: William Messing; used with permission from BigStockPhoto.com.

p. 16: *Hair* logo and artwork copyright Michael Butler; used with permission.

p. 21: Photo Copyright Michael Butler; used with permission.

p. 24: Alex Bramwell; used with permission from BigStockPhoto.com.

2/India from a Child's Eyes

pp. 26, 28, 30, 31: photos from Caryl Matrisiciana's personal collection.

p. 33: Vladislav Lebedinski; used with permission from BigStockPhoto.com.

p. 34: top: Joe Scarangella; used with permission from BigStockPhoto.com.
bottom: Duncan Walker; used with permission from iStockPhoto.com.

3/Living in a Paradox

p. 39: Public domain; from *Compendium of Illustrations*; Hindu potter, Lahore, India; *Indika*.

p. 41: Public domain; from *Compendium of Illustrations*; *Century Magazine*.

p. 46: top: Jeremy Edwards; used with permission from iStockPhoto.com.
bottom: Max Beaton; used with permission from BigStockPhoto.com.

4/Milestones in Madness

p. 49. S M M A Rizvi; used with permission from BigStockPhoto.com

p 50, 53: photo from Caryl Matrisiciana's personal collection.

p. 52: Arlene Gee; used with permission from BigStockPhoto.com.

5/Landing in the Butter

p. 60: Dean Tomlinson; used with permission from iStockPhoto.com.

p. 62: Nic Taylor; used with permission from iStockPhoto.com.

6/In Search of the Lost Chord

p. 72: Graça Victoria; used with permission from BigStockPhoto.com.

p. 80: Clemente do Rosario/PhotoShelter; used with permission from www.PhotoShelter.com.

8/A New Heart

p. 88: Nicholas Sutcliffe; used with permission from BigStockPhoto.com.

p. 98: Jennifer Ruch; used with permission from iStockPhoto.com.

10/In the Land of the Guru

p. 124: Public domain; from *Compendium of Illustrations;* Taj Mahal, Uttar Pradesh, India; *Incredible Structures.*

p. 126: Michal Sosna; used with permission from 123rf.com.

p. 127: Richard Robinson; used with permission from BigStockPhoto.com.

p. 131: Sathish V J; used with permission from iStockPhoto.com.

11/Aquarian Fairs—East and West

p. 140 top: Jeremy Roberts; used with permission from BigStockPhoto. com. middle: Sunil Kumar used with permission from 123rf.com. bottom: Jeremy Roberts; used with permission from BigStockPhoto.com.

p. 148: Holger Mette, used with permission from BigStockPhoto.com.

p. 149: Oksana Perkins; used with permission from iStockPhoto.com.

14/Yoga Uncoiled

p. 181: Ron Riesterer/PhotoShelter; used with permission from www. PhotoShelter.com.

p. 183: Iofoto; used with permission from 123rf.com.

p. 184: Christos Georghiou; used with permission from BigStockPhoto.com.

15/The New (Age) Christian

p. 194: Paul Giamou; used with permission from iStockPhoto.com.

16/ "The Dawning of the Age"

p. 215: Mahesh; used with permission from iStockPhoto.com.

Border through book: Public domain; from *Compendium of Illustrations.*

Cover Photos:

Background: Melaney Kakkar; used with permission from BigStock-Photo.com. border-Mehndi Arch: Heidi Priesnitz; used with permission from iStockPhoto.com. background: Konstantin Kalishko; used with permission from BigStockPhoto.com. sunrise: Alexander Briel Perez; used with permission from BigStockPhoto.com. Girl meditating: Alex Bramwell; used with permission from BigStockPhoto.com.

Lyric Credits

Index

Note: Because of their frequent use in this book, certain terms like Hinduism, New Age, and India are not in this Index.